Ships and Seafaring in ancient times

LIONEL CASSON

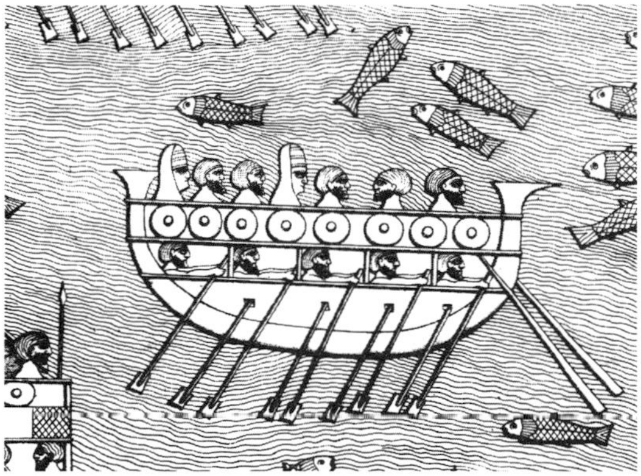

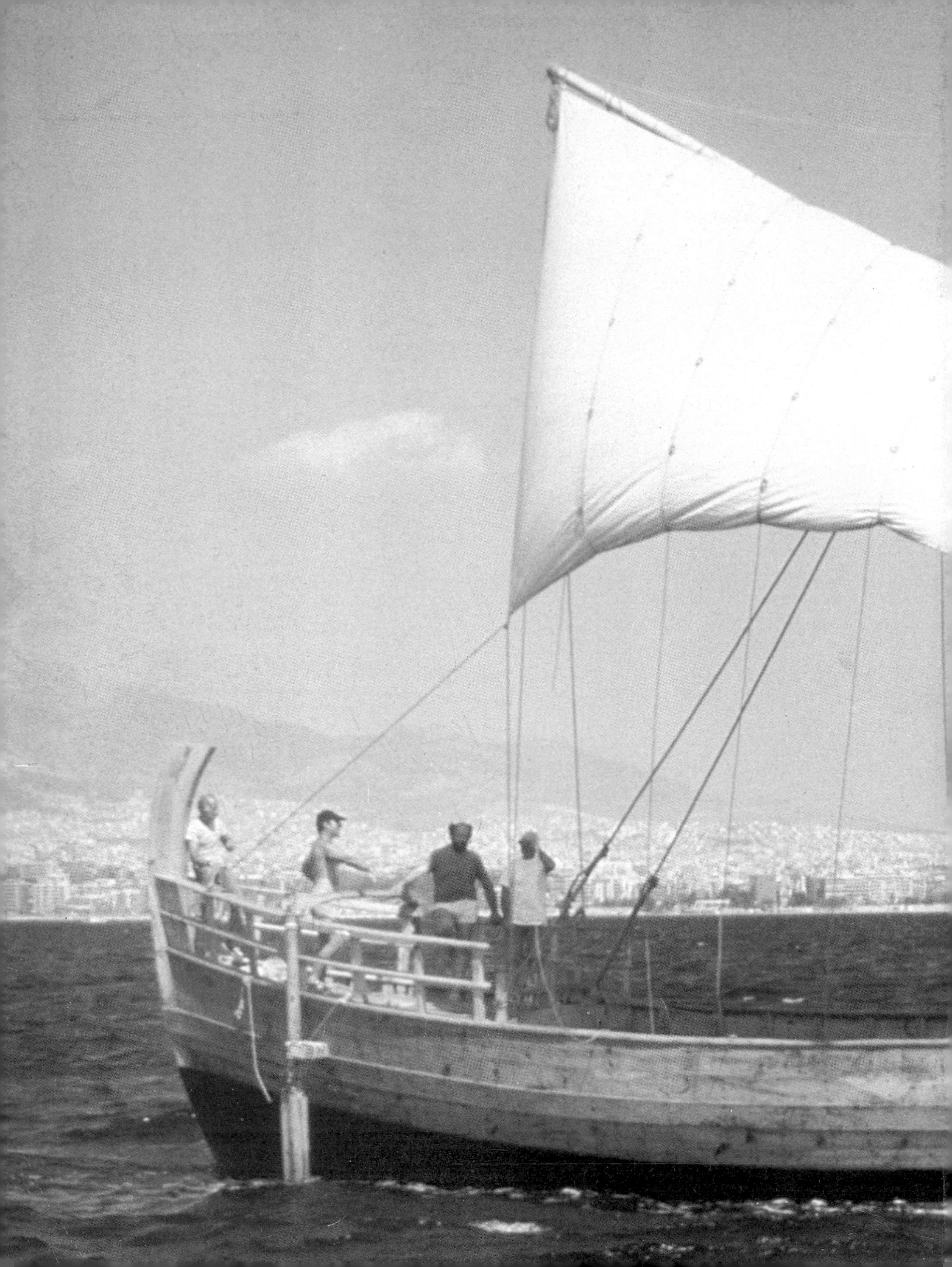

Ships and Seafaring in ancient times

LIONEL CASSON

UNIVERSITY OF TEXAS PRESS

International Standard Book
Number 0-292-71162-x
Library of Congress Catalog
Card Number 93-61490

Second University of Texas Press
printing, 1996

Printed in Great Britain

Designed by Roger Davies

HALF-TITLE PAGE Phoenician galley. Detail of Fig. 33.

TITLE PAGE *Kyrenia II*, replica of a small Greek merchantman of about 300 BC, under sail.

THIS PAGE A scene from the Bayeux tapestry, depicting one of William the Conqueror's ships transporting horses as well as men. Eleventh century AD.

Contents

1

The Birth of the Boat

New Zealand aborigines paddle over lakes astride bundles of reeds. Iraqi herdsmen cross streams on inflated goatskins. Tamil natives fish by drifting along with a log under the arms, while Sindhi natives fish lying prone over open-mouthed pots. Devices like these were no doubt the earliest forms of water transport, pressed into use by ancient primitive peoples living along lakes and rivers. Simple, convenient and readily available, they have maintained their usefulness in undeveloped areas to this day.

There came a time when mere floats were not enough, when travellers sought something that would not only buoy them up but keep them out of the water as well, even allow them to venture onto the open sea. The first step in this direction was the creation of rafts, which fully met these needs and had the additional virtue of accommodating more than a single person. In places where trees grew, they would have been the type that has become most familiar, of bound logs. Along the Nile or in the marshy lower stretches of the Tigris and Euphrates, where wood is scarce but reeds are abundant, they were very likely made of batches of reed bundles 2
tied together.

In certain areas ordinary rafts cannot be used. The Tigris and Euphrates, for example, along their upper reaches in Armenia, run with a swift current over many stony rapids, a combination that can easily shatter a log raft. From earliest times they were vital arteries, for they flowed down into and through Mesopotamia, the birthplace of civilisation. To exploit them the inhabitants devised buoyed rafts, specifically the type consisting 4
of a wooden frame supported by inflated animal skins. Quite possibly they got the idea by observing people crossing the rivers on such skins: 3
the sight could well have triggered the thought that, if one bladder could hold up the weight of one person, a batch of them set under a platform could hold up the weight not only of several people but also of whatever they happened to be carrying. This form of buoyed raft was ideal for rivers with rapids. The sharp rocks might cause a blow-out or two, but, with the rest of the bladders intact, that was hardly serious – and even the punctured ones could be patched in short order. In addition, it offered a ready-made solution for the problem that afflicts all who float down rivers: how to get back against the current. Herodotus, the keen-eyed, keen-minded Greek who has been called Father of History but could equally well be called Father of the Travelogue, visited Babylon on the lower Euphrates around the middle of the fifth century BC and describes how raftsmen who came there from the north got themselves home. 'Each raft', he writes, 'has aboard a live donkey, the larger ones several. After arriving at Babylon and disposing of their cargo, the men auction off the wooden frame, load the bladders on the donkeys, and walk back to Armenia.'[1]

Where there were no rapids to traverse, rafts could be buoyed by a line of pots, which, though clumsier than bladders, had the advantage of

1 Heracles sails to the Garden of the Hesperides in a pot boat. From an Athenian vase in the Vatican Museum, about 480 BC.

Numbers in the margins refer to illustrations. Colour plates are indicated by Roman numerals.

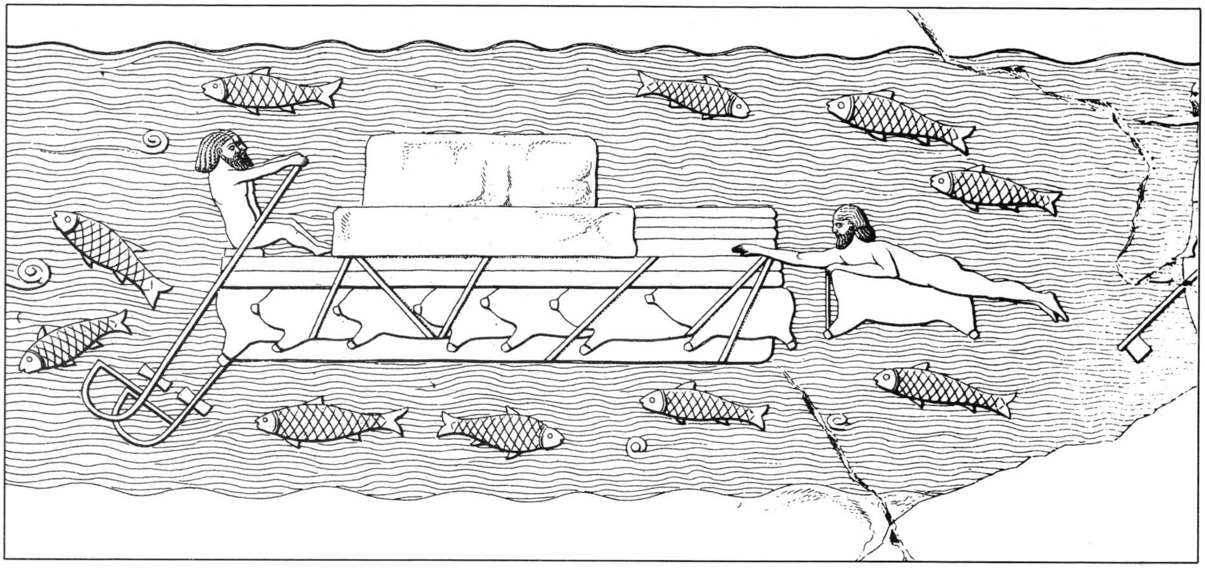

2 LEFT Assyrian soldiers in a boat-shaped raft of bundles of reeds hunt down enemies in the marshes at the mouth of the Tigris and Euphrates. Relief from the palace of Sennacherib (704–681 BC) at Nineveh, now in the British Museum.

3 BELOW LEFT Two Assyrian soldiers buoyed by inflated skins swim to the safety of a fortress; they were evidently in a hurry to blow up the skins, for they still have the mouthpieces between their lips. Relief from the palace of Ashurnasirpal II (883–859 BC) at Nimrud, now in the British Museum.

4 ABOVE Assyrians transporting stone on a raft buoyed by inflated skins. Drawn from a relief in the palace of Sennacherib (704–681 BC).

being cheaper. The Greeks had such rafts at least as early as the sixth
century BC, for carved on gems of that date are pictures of Heracles 6
lolling at his ease on a pot-buoyed raft as he heads toward one of his labours. From historical times there are reports indicating that they could attain considerable size; in 252 BC, for example, a Roman commander transported a troop of 140 or so war elephants over the Strait of Messina on them.

Floats and rafts were preliminaries. The crucial step in the development of water transport was the creation of the boat, the device that keeps travellers and cargo not only out of the water but dry as well.

One of the earliest forms of boat could well have been the skin boat, fashioned by stretching hides over a light frame of branches and lacing them together with withies, cords or thongs. All one needed to produce it was a flint knife and bone needle. It could be made in any size required – small and light enough to be packed on the back when not in use or big and commodious enough to accommodate several tons of cargo. Assyrian reliefs of about 700 BC show that the boatmen of the lower Euphrates
were by that time using round skin boats – coracles, to give them their 5
technical name – that had the size and strength to carry chariots or massive loads of building stone. Herodotus saw coracles when he paid his visit to the area, and they were still to be seen right up to this century. Another place where skin boats were favoured was the British Isles. Julius Caesar evidently became well acquainted with the versions used there during his invasion of England in 55 BC, for, when in the Roman civil wars half a decade later he needed to get his soldiers across some river in Spain, he ordered the men 'to make boats of the kind his experience in Britain years before had taught him. The keel and ribs were made first, out of light wood; then the rest of the body of the craft was made

5 Assyrians transporting a load of stone in a coracle; in the water two men fish – very successfully – astride inflated skins. Relief from the palace of Sennacherib (704–681 BC), now in the British Museum.

of wickerwork and covered with skins.'[2] What he had seen and was reproducing were perhaps curraghs rather than coracles, craft of skins that, instead of being round, are shaped like true boats with a prow and stern.

The cheapest form of primitive boat was the pot boat, simply a clay container large enough to accommodate a passenger. But, like the pot-buoyed raft, it was strictly for places free of rocks. The ancient Egyptians, for example, found pot boats ideal for getting around the marshy waterways of the Nile delta. The Greeks used them as well; there are pictures on Greek vases showing Heracles voyaging in a hero-sized pot. 1

Mesopotamia turned to coracles and Egypt to pot boats because in both regions trees were scarce and wood as a consequence was expensive. Where trees were plentiful the earliest boats were undoubtedly bark canoes and dugouts. Perhaps the bark canoe came first, for it can be made without tools: all that is needed is a trough-like length of bark and two lumps of clay to stop up the ends. The dugout requires more, but 7
not too much, a stone cutting tool (or even just a hard shell) or the controlled use of fire and lots of patience. In ancient times we can trace the dugout chronologically from the Stone Age to the end of antiquity and geographically from Spain to India, wherever there were forests to supply the logs.

6 Heracles sails on a raft buoyed by pots. Carved Etruscan gem, 6th century BC.

A common way of adapting a dugout for use on open water is to provide protection against waves by adding planks, set on edge, along each side, with ribs running athwartship to brace them. Here we have in embryo the fundamental elements – keel, ribs (or frames, as they are known in nautical terminology) and strakes – of the planked boat, the basic form of boat from ancient times to the present. There is good reason to think that at least one avenue that led to the planked boat was by way of the dugout; that, in the course of time, so many planks had been added to the sides, one atop the other, that they came to form what we can properly call a hull, while the original dugout had shrunk in the process to the dimensions of a keel. Just when this took place is hard to say. The earliest planked boats that we know of come from Old Kingdom Egypt, but the development there, as we shall see, seems to have followed a different course.

How did the primitive shipbuilders add the side planking to their dugouts? In other words, what sort of fastening did they use? Here again, it is hard to give a sure answer, but certain straws in the wind indicate that at least one way was by sewing them with fibres, cords or thongs. The idea of a boat made up of planks sewn together seems strange. Actually, it is a type that has been in wide use in many parts of the world 8
and in some places still is. In the Indian Ocean it dominated the waters right up to the fifteenth century, when the arrival of the Portuguese opened the area to European methods. A Greek sea captain or merchant who wrote in the first century AD reports the use of small sewn boats off Zanzibar and the southern coast of Arabia. Marco Polo saw sewn boats at Hormuz at the entrance to the Persian Gulf. He took a dim view of them: they were

> wretched affairs and many get lost; for they have no iron fastenings and are only stitched together with twine made from the husk of the Indian nut. They beat this husk until it becomes like horse-hair and from this they spin

7 Dugout of oak, 46 feet (*c.* 14 m) long, found near Ferrara. National Archaeological Museum, Ferrara, 4th–5th century AD.

8 Interior of a modern sewn boat on the beach at Madras. Note that the cords pass over a packing of caulking material to ensure the watertightness of the seam; the ancients used the very same technique.

twine and with it stitch the planks of the ships together. It keeps well and is not corroded by sea-water but it will not stand well in a storm.[3]

Later travellers report seeing large sewn boats, of 40 to 60 tons' burden, and versions of fair size were still plying the waters of East Africa and around Sri Lanka in the early decades of this century.

The earliest surviving example of a sewn boat, as we shall see, was found beside the great pyramid of Giza, but it is unquestionably a descendant of ancestors that go back to Egypt's primitive times. Sewn boats are mentioned by ancient Roman writers, from tragic poets to the compiler of Rome's standard encyclopaedia, in ways betraying their conviction that such boats belonged to the distant past, the days of the Trojan War, of Aeneas and Odysseus. They were surely right in connecting the sewn boat with an early age. They were wrong only in assuming that it had not lived on: marine archaeologists have found remains of sewn boats that date from the sixth century BC on into the Roman Imperial age.

But the fashioning of a hull by sewing planks together, despite its early appearance and continued existence, remained a byway. As the following chapters will reveal, the mainstream of boatbuilding followed a different channel.

2
Egypt

Civilisation arose in Mesopotamia and Egypt, helped by the presence of great rivers, in the one case the Tigris and Euphrates and in the other the Nile. But only the Nile played a significant role in the history of water transport.

The rivers of Mesopotamia had limited use as waterways. Not only are the northern stretches rocky and shallow but the prevailing wind of the region blows from the north, the same direction as the current; until the development of the steamboat, vessels got upstream only through the laborious process of being towed by teams trudging along the bank. It is 9
no surprise that, except for the floats and coracles mentioned above, the area produced merely undistinguished small craft.

The Nile, on the other hand, is a perfect waterway, offering a broad and clear run of some 500 miles from the beginning of the delta near Cairo to the First Cataract at Aswan. Moreover, since the prevailing wind, although from the north as in Mesopotamia, here blows against the flow of the water, the river offers an easy ride both ways: boatmen drift downstream or, if the wind is particularly strong, run out the oars to help the current move them; when ready to return, they raise sail and get wafted back home. It is no surprise that the inhabitants of the valley of the Nile, with so convenient a stream linking their whole land, not only created craft of many varieties and sizes but were the first in recorded history to use that prime nautical device, the sail.

They did have to put up with one shortcoming: few trees grew in their homeland and none that yielded good ship-timber. The most common was the acacia, whose wood is brittle and comes in but short lengths; in time the Egyptian shipwrights worked out ways to utilise it. But, if wood was scarce, reeds were abundant – the celebrated bulrushes from which the infant Moses' cradle was fashioned – and for their first water transport it was to these that they turned. By the middle of the fourth millennium BC the Egyptians were building rafts of bundles of reeds tied together, and in the course of the next few centuries they introduced improve-

9 Assyrian hauliers towing a boat. Bronze band from the gates of the palace of Shalmaneser III (858–824 BC) at Balawat, now in the British Museum.

10 Nineteenth-century log canoe of the Cameroons with a frond in the bows as a sail.

11 ABOVE RIGHT Egyptian raft of bundles of reeds fitted with pole mast and square sail, depicted on a Predynastic vase in the British Museum. About 3500 BC.

ments. They learned to shape them, making them long and narrow and gracefully bowed. They learned to fashion paddles to propel them and to mount paddles on the quarters to serve as rudders. They learned to build craft big enough to accommodate a pair of deck cabins and to require a long line of paddlers to move them.

Then the Egyptians took an epoch-making step, becoming the first people to exploit a source of energy other than human or animal muscle – they learned how to harness the wind to propel these craft. The Egyptians started by doing what primitive boatmen were still doing up to recent times, by setting up a leafy frond in the bows. It worked only when the 10
wind was blowing from astern and hardly very efficiently then, but the sight of a boat moving without being paddled must have seemed as miraculous thirty-two centuries before the beginning of the Christian Era as that of a steamboat did eighteen centuries after. Improvement came quickly: by about 3500 BC the Egyptians had replaced this improvised sail with a true one, a square probably of woven reeds or leaves set on a 11
vertical mast stepped far forward in the bows. A squaresail necessarily has a spar – the yard, as it is called – along the head from which it hangs; no doubt these earliest versions had yards, although the representations are too roughly drawn to show them.

In the next two millennia there was continued development – a development that can be closely followed, thanks to the predilection of Egypt's royalty and nobility for burial in elaborate tombs and to the country's perennially dry climate, which has enabled these tombs to survive through the ages. For it was customary to adorn the walls with paintings, which often included scenes of the funeral procession that bore the deceased to burial across the river. These conveniently illustrate for us several kinds of boats: those manned by multiple paddlers or rowers, which did the I
towing; the elaborate one that bore the coffin; those that carried the III
victims for the sacrifice and other necessities for the funeral ceremony;

and those that carried the relatives and friends who took part in the ceremony. Other scenes show the mystic voyage of the soul to the other world, and boats appear here too, since this was conceived as taking place on the river. Still other scenes deal with daily life, and these sometimes show boats, such as the portrayals of the deceased fishing or hunting in 12, IV
the marshes. The objects placed inside the tomb often include little 16, III
models of boats. And – a unique discovery – in a sealed stone trench alongside the biggest of the mighty pyramids at Giza, the one erected by Cheops about 2550 BC, archaeologists found an actual boat; it had been deposited there, dismantled for easy stowing, as part of the pharaoh's funerary furniture, and the restorers were able to reassemble it. Thanks to the tomb illustrations, the models, Cheops' boat and a few others that have been unearthed, we are better informed about the water transport of ancient Egypt from roughly 3000 to 1000 BC than of any other place or time in antiquity.

The material that dates from Old Kingdom times, *c.* 2700–2200 BC, reveals that Egyptian shipwrights had very soon learned to improve the reed raft. They now made it in the shape of a boat, with a graceful spoon- 12
like form and a prow and stern that came together into a point, often finished off with an ornament resembling a lotus bud. Light and shallow and manoeuvrable, reed craft were ideal for nosing through the streams of the marshes that lined parts of the river or for plying the innumerable canals that branched off from it.

But the Egyptians needed a good deal more than something that could traverse marshes and canals. By 3000 BC they had begun to build tombs of stone, and the stone often had to be transported from the quarry to the site by water. The massive blocks of fine limestone, for example, that at Giza formed the outer facing of the two biggest pyramids and part of the third, came from across the river, while one of the temples nearby was of granite cut from outcrops at Aswan, hundreds of miles upstream. Very likely the need for vessels that could handle such ponderous cargoes was what led Egyptian shipwrights to the use of wood.

Their first boats in the new material were square at each end, more barge than boat, no doubt because the shape was easier for inexperienced carpenters. They learned quickly; soon they were replicating in wood the II
graceful form of the reed craft. Since Egypt, as mentioned above, lacks trees to provide good timber, they worked out a special technique that enabled them to make do with what was available. Herodotus, whose travels included a visit to Egypt, describes it:

> The boats they use for carrying cargo are made from the acacia tree .... From this acacia tree they cut planks three feet long, which they put together like courses of brick, building up the hull as follows: they join these three-foot planks together by means of long, close-set tenons; when they have built up a hull in this fashion [out of the planks], they stretch crossbeams over them. They do not use frames.[1]

12 Harpooning hippopotami from reed boats. The master stands immobile holding his harpoon, while servants on another boat poise for the cast. Relief in a tomb at Saqqara. About 2400 BC.

This was, to be sure, the way it was done when he was there, in the middle of the fifth century BC, but pictures in tombs and the remains of several boats reveal that the procedure had been the same for millennia. Today we build wooden hulls by making a skeleton of keel and frames (ribs) and then clothing this with a skin of planking. The Egyptian shipwright dispensed with the skeleton and launched straight into building up a shell of planking. He laid down a centre plank – which was the closest thing his boat would have to a keel – and then he added planks, edge to edge, on either side, fastening them to each other. When the planks, built up in this fashion, reached the desired height and the hull was complete, he stretched crossbeams from one gunwale to the other; these, besides supporting any deck planking, kept the sides from sagging outward. Since he had to work with short lengths of wood, the centre plank and the other lines of planking were made up of these short lengths 13 fastened end to end. The vessel discovered alongside Cheops' pyramid was basically a version of the sewn boat, for its planks were fastened by cutting slots near their edges and inserting into these cords that bound 14 plank to plank; the cords ran over, and thereby held in place, battens that, set over the seams on the inside, helped keep these watertight. In several other craft that have survived and date somewhat later, about 2000 BC, the fastening consisted, as Herodotus describes, of mortise and tenon joints in the edges and ends of the planks. Herodotus is not quite right in implying that frames were never used; they were never used in the consistent manner he was accustomed to in Greek lands, but Egyptian shipwrights did at times insert them.

The Egyptian technique produced hulls that were not very strong but were adequate for plying the waters of a river. Craft of any size were decked, and this provided added strength. Cabins were set upon the deck – on cargo carriers a mere shelter aft, on passenger vessels usually an ample structure; the cabins were generally lightly built, consisting of a 11 frame with a covering of mats. The biggest ships, despite being rivercraft, attained impressive size. Cheops' boat, for example, was an elegantly slender vessel almost 150 feet (45 m) from stem to stern (the shipwrights, employees of the pharaoh who erected for himself Egypt's mightiest pyramid, did not have to put up with short bits of the native acacia but had at their disposal timbers of cedar, some of them 60 feet (18 m) long, imported from Lebanon). The barges that carried the granite obelisks from the quarries at Aswan down-river to the places where they were erected were not only long but broad as well. Queen Hatshepsut, who reigned as pharaoh around 1500 BC, included in the reliefs decorating her tomb a picture of the veritable behemoth she had her shipwrights 15 design to transport the two lofty obelisks, each almost 100 feet (30 m) high, that she set up at Karnak. The estimates of its dimensions give it a length of some 200 feet (60 m) and a beam of some 70 (21 m); it was, in other words, broader and longer than Nelson's *Victory*. To provide the

13 ABOVE Egyptian boatwrights building up the shell of a hull out of short lengths of planking. Drawn from a relief in a tomb at Beni Hasan. About 2000 BC.

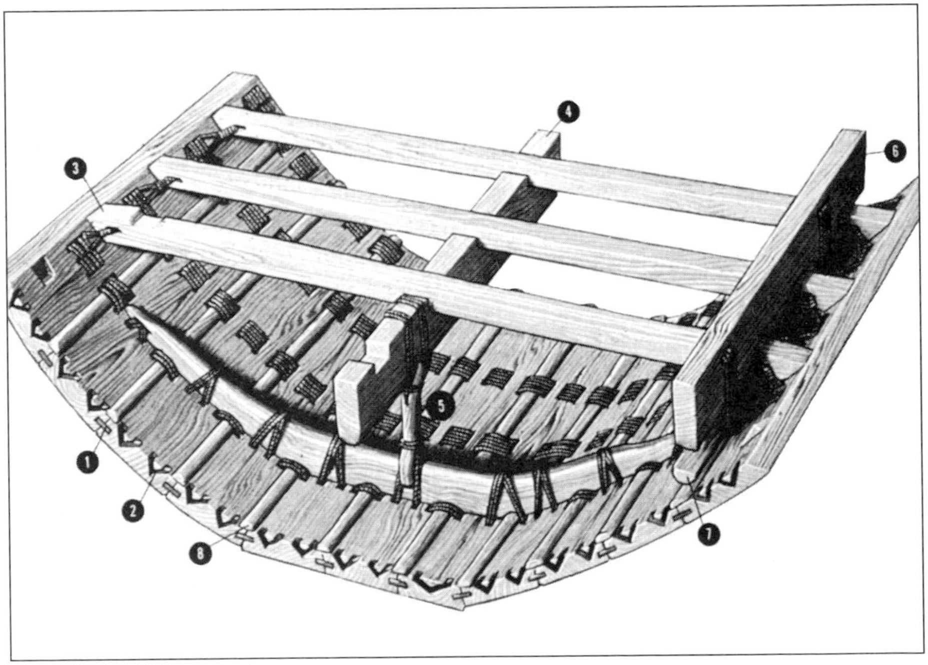

14 Sketch illustrating the system of joinery and sewing used in the Cheops boat: (1) mortise and tenon joint, (2) V-shaped slot through which the sewing cords pass, (3) deck beam, (4) central fore-and-aft timber, (5) support for it, (6) side fore-and-aft timber, (7) member for holding its lashings, (8) battens, held in place by the cords, to ensure the watertightness of the seams.

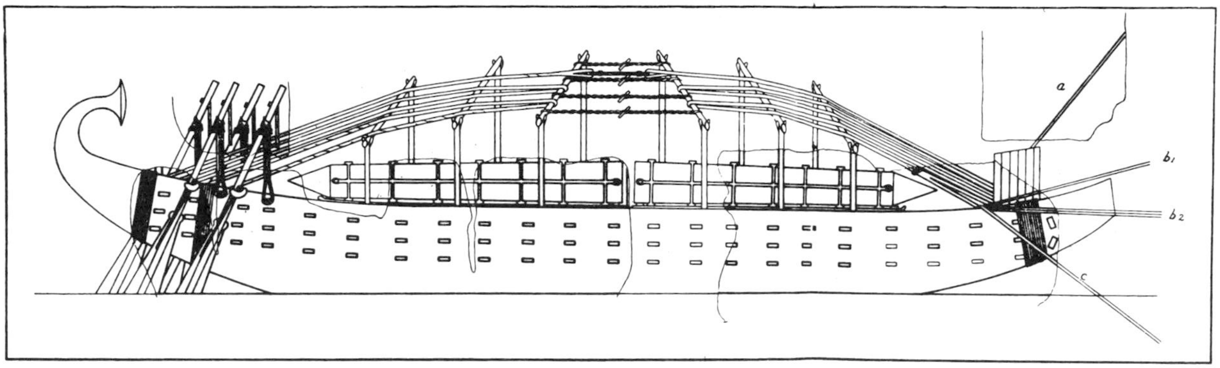

15 A massive Egyptian barge loaded with two obelisks quarried at Aswan near the First Cataract being towed downstream to Karnak. Note the elaborate rope truss that keeps the ends from sagging and the three lines of deck beams to provide the strength to support the ponderous load. The lines marked *a*, *b*, *c* are tow-lines leading to the flotilla of galleys that did the pulling. Drawn from a relief on the tomb of Hatshepsut at Deir-el-Bahri. About 1500 BC.

strength it needed to bear up under a load of about 700 tons the shipwrights fitted it with three rows of crossbeams instead of a single row. In addition, they rigged a powerful truss to keep the ends from sagging, a set of heavy ropes that they lashed about one end, ran over uprights the length of the vessel, and lashed about the other end. It took a flotilla of twenty-seven oar-driven tugs, each manned by thirty rowers, to tow this mammoth.

The Egyptians for many centuries used only paddles. Long slender craft were moved by teams of paddlers lining the sides. Soon after 2500 BC, however, rowing replaced paddling, which thereafter was limited to small craft. Vertical pins (tholepins) were set in the gunwales, and each oar, secured to its thole by a leather or rope circlet, pivoted about it. The Egyptians used oars that were short and set at a relatively steep angle; as a consequence, pulling on them was strenuous work. Like the men who manned the great sweeps of the Mediterranean galleys in the sixteenth to the eighteenth centuries, Egyptian rowers first rose to their feet in order to dip the blade into the water and then delivered the stroke by throwing themselves back on the bench. The standard rowing garb was a short kilt, and since the repeated fall on the bench was hard on the seat of their kilts, they sewed a patch of leather there to serve as chafing gear; Egyptian artists, scrupulously attentive to detail, include this homely touch in their pictures. Steering was done by means of oversize oars mounted on the quarters; often there was more than one, and big craft II
could have as many as five. At first the helmsmen just clutched the end of the shaft with both hands but, after 2500 BC, a tiller bar for them to hold was socketed into it, and this must have made steering much easier. Smaller craft could have a single steering oar mounted on a vertical pole 16, I
at the stern, and, as time went on, this system became increasingly popular.

Some boats were made to be paddled or rowed, others carried sail in addition, and still others were sailing craft pure and simple.

The earliest sail, as we noted, was square and hung on a pole mast set 11
far up in the bows. Soon a bipod form of mast, with one leg planted on each gunwale, came into use. It suited both reed and wooden boats, for II

neither had a keel into which the heel of a pole mast could be securely socketed. The sail was tall and narrow, a shape that was particularly useful for catching the upper breezes when going through those reaches where the Nile flows between high-rising cliffs; the lateen sails of modern Nile craft are tall and slender for the same reason. Masts were supported not only by forestays and backstays but also by multiple lines running 11
more or less aft, which may have served as shrouds. The sail not only has a yard, that is, a spar along the head, but also – a typical Egyptian feature – a second spar (a boom) along the foot. On small craft the sails were probably made of papyrus, on larger craft of linen, not one piece but horizontal bands sewn together. Neither material was able to bear unaided the weight of the boom, which must have been heavy since men are often shown standing on it, so this was held up by a network of lines 18
fastened at intervals along its length and converging at the upper part of the mast. The boom remained fixed; sail was raised or furled by hauling up or lowering the yard. Running rigging included a halyard for hoisting yard and sail, braces made fast to the yard-arms to swivel the sail to port or starboard, and sheets made fast to the ends of the boom to trim the sail. All the running rigging was handled by sheer muscle, since ancient Egypt never learned the use of the block and tackle; the halyard, for example, simply passed through a hole near the tip of the mast. The lines were of palm or papyrus fibres or of various grasses. Despite the loftiness and complexity of the rig, it was retractable; when not needed, the sail 17
was furled and the mast was unstepped and laid out on the deck.

16 Egyptian sailing craft of about 1900 BC, with a pole mast stepped amidships. Ancient model in the British Museum.

Bipod masts did not last much beyond 2200 BC. After that all boats had pole masts. The position of the mast changed over the years: well forward in earliest times, it gradually moved aft until, by 1900 BC or so, it reached amidships, and there it stayed. Probably the shift was connected 16
with a growing awareness that winds other than one from dead astern could be utilised, that a sail set amidships and braced round to the proper slant can do just as well with a wind from over the quarter. About 2000 BC the tall narrow sail gave way to its very opposite, a short and wide one; it was, however, carried high on the mast.

The vast majority of the images of boats that have survived from Egypt are of rivercraft. Luckily there are also a few depictions of the ships built for use on the open water.

Pharaoh Sahure, who ruled about 2475 BC, sent a fleet from the coast of Egypt across the lower corner of the Mediterranean to the Levant. He was so proud of the achievement that he included a picture of the arrival 17
of the vessels back home among the reliefs decorating his mortuary temple, and thereby furnished us with the oldest clear representations of seagoing ships. The hulls, long and slender and with overhangs fore and aft, reflect the spoon-like shape of contemporary rivercraft and were constructed the same way, with no keel and few frames. That was adequate for a river but not the sea, and so the Egyptians, to provide the

17 Egyptian seagoing vessels of about 2450 BC. Like contemporary rivercraft, they have a bipod mast. Unlike them, they have a heavy rope truss to keep the ends from sagging. Relief on the pyramid of Sahure at Abusir.

needed strength, introduced an all-important feature, a rope truss, the ancestor of the truss that appears on the barge made to transport Hatshepsut's obelisks. A heavy rope cable was lashed around the prow, carried from there over a line of forked sticks the length of the vessel, and then lashed about the stern. A lever thrust between the strands amidships enabled the crew to twist it like a tourniquet and, by twisting and twisting, to arrive at the tension needed to keep the ends from sagging. The vessels were propelled by both oars and sail. The rig was the same as that of contemporary rivercraft, a tall narrow sail set on a bipod mast that, when the ship proceeded under oars, could be unstepped and laid out on deck. Steering was done by three steering oars on each quarter.

The next representations of seagoing ships date from a thousand years 18
later. We owe them to the same pharaoh who provided the invaluable picture of an obelisk barge, Queen Hatshepsut. One of her major acts was the sending of an expedition from some port on the Red Sea to a region the Egyptians called Punt, either the Ethiopian shore of the Red Sea or the coast of Somalia further along. She commemorated it in a series of reliefs on a wall of her tomb. In a lower register we see the arrival at Punt: two galleys, having reached the quay, have lowered sail and are ready to tie up, while three others, their great sails bellying in the wind and their rowers pulling on the oars, are heading into the harbour. In an upper register we see the departure: some vessels are still loading, with stevedores trudging up the gangplanks, while others, fully loaded, are moving off under sail and oar. The text in hieroglyphs that accompanies the pictures not only identifies the items of cargo – ebony, myrrh, ivory, gold, even 'a southern panther alive, captured for Her Majesty'[2] – but records what some of the participants are saying: 'Hard to port!' calls out a pilot; 'Watch your step!' shouts a stevedore.

The vessels are in shape like those of Sahure's fleet but have cleaner, more graceful lines, and the stern, instead of ending in a straight post, makes a sweeping curve finished off with the age-old lotus bud ornament. There are fifteen rowers along each side; allowing the standard amount of room, 3 feet, for each, the space they occupied was 45 feet (13.7 m) and, since the foredecks and poopdecks are ample, the overall length may have come up to 90 feet. Steering has been simplified: a single oversize oar on each quarter has replaced the multiple oars of earlier craft. The ships must have been built in the usual Egyptian fashion with little internal stiffening, for they are all equipped with the anti-sagging truss. The rig is like that on the rivercraft of this age, a pole mast set amidships and on it a sail far wider than tall – so wide that the yard is made of two tapering spars lashed together at the thick ends. The short mast, not requiring the elaborate staying of its lofty bipod predecessors, lacks their cluster of lines running aft and is held up simply by two forestays and a single backstay. The boom along the foot, as heavy as

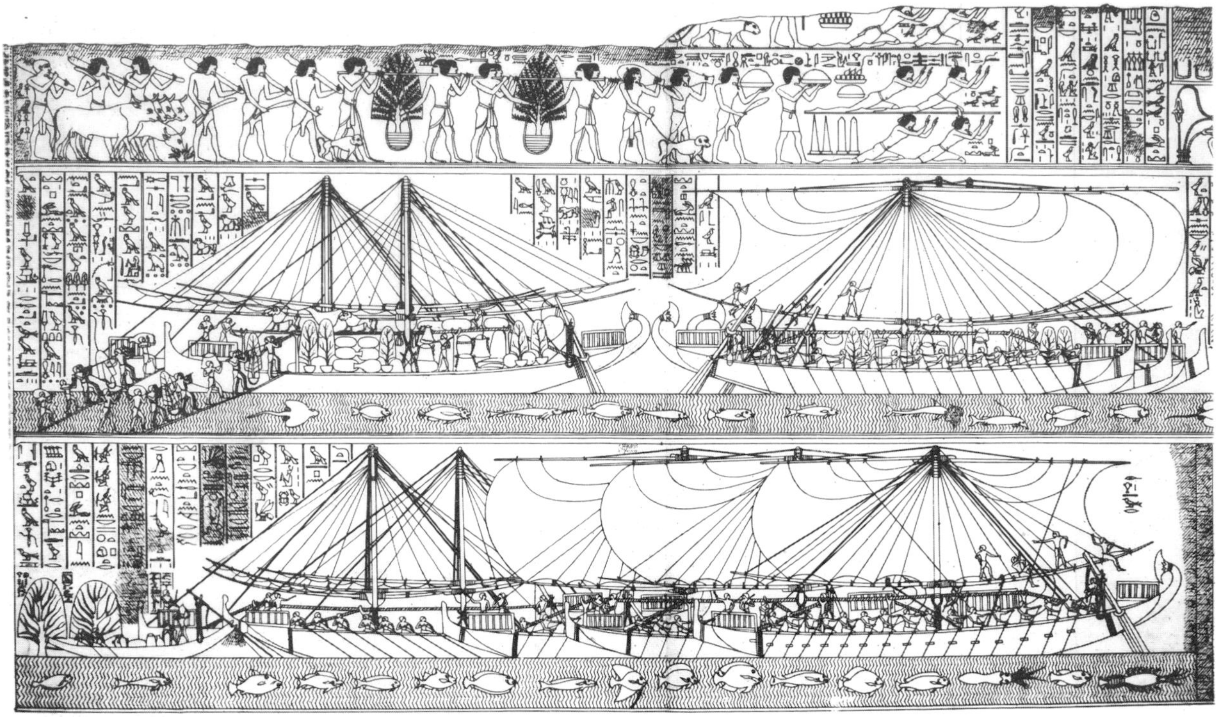

19 The Egyptian fleet of Ramses III repels an attempt at invasion. This is the only representation of an identifiable sea battle that has survived from ancient times. Ramses' vessels have curved hulls and low stems and sterns; the enemy vessels have angular hulls with straight stemposts and sternposts. The sails of the Egyptian craft, like those of the enemy, do not have booms. Drawn from a relief on the temple of Ramses III at Medinet Habu. About 1190 BC.

18 Fleet of Egyptian seagoing vessels of about 1500 BC. Like contemporary rivercraft, they have pole masts and sails that are broader than high and stiffened by booms along the foot. Drawn from a relief on the tomb of Hatshepsut at Deir-el-Bahri.

ever, is supported by the usual network of lifts. The yard is raised by two halyards, which, being secured to the quarters, reinforce the single backstay. Neither on Sahure's craft nor on these is there any gear visible for shortening sail. Indeed, it is hard to see how the Egyptian squaresail, with its foot stretched along a spar, could be shortened. Perhaps, as on the Mediterranean lateen-rigged craft of later ages, when the wind made up, the crews stripped off the working sail and replaced it with a smaller one.

Another unique series of pictures, dating from 300 years later, supplies the final chapter in the history of the development of Egyptian ships. The decades just before and after 1200 BC were troubled times for the Egyptians. A wave of invading peoples washed over the eastern Mediterranean and the lands around it and lapped at their very shores. There it was stopped by the army and fleet of Ramses III. He celebrated his victory by carving on the wall of a temple he erected near Thebes an account of the struggle, along with a series of monumental reliefs illus- 19
trating it. These include the earliest complete representation that we have of a sea battle – indeed, the only representation of an identifiable historical sea battle that has survived from ancient times. The enemy fleet had got as far as the mouth of the Nile, and somehow Ramses managed to catch it there off guard (see Chapter 5). The Egyptian galleys, their oarsmen pulling hard and their marines firing showers of arrows, storm in among the invaders' ships, which lie motionless in the water with their sails furled and the oars stowed away out of sight. Enemy dead hang over the ships' sides; enemy corpses float in the water; one enemy ship has capsized.

The artists have carefully distinguished the vessels of the two fleets. The invaders' ships are angular, with straight stempost and sternpost, both ending in a bird's head as ornament. They are totally dissimilar from those of the Egyptians, which have a curved hull and low prow and stern. Comparison of these with the ships in Hatshepsut's reliefs reveals that important changes have taken place during the intervening three centuries. The hull is shorter and heavier. Stem and stern are treated in a new way: the elegant curved stern with lotus-bud tip of the earlier craft has been replaced by a simple undecorated sloping stern, and the straight stempost by a simple projection ending in a lion's head. And – a most significant change – the anti-sagging truss has disappeared; Egyptian shipbuilders have switched from their traditional technique to one that provided enough internal strength to do without that hitherto essential feature. Egypt, at least so far as its warcraft are concerned, had joined the Mediterranean mainstream.

3

Ancient Shipbuilding

Some twenty-five miles south of Giza lies Dahshur, site of a cluster of pyramids, one of which was put up by Pharaoh Sesostris III, who reigned from 1878 to 1843 BC. In 1894 excavators found alongside it the hulls of six boats, fully preserved. This discovery revealed the procedure followed by Egyptian shipwrights as explained in the previous chapter. But what of the inhabitants of the other ancient lands around the Mediterranean, particularly maritime peoples, such as the Phoenicians and Greeks? How did they build their boats? Until the middle of this century, we had no idea.

There were clues, but they went unrecognised. As far back as 1864 part of the hull of a Roman ship had been unearthed on the site of Marseilles' ancient harbour, and it was noted that its planks were fastened to each other with mortise and tenon joints, a practice totally unknown to European shipwrights. In 1896 a scholar with expertise in maritime matters published an article that in effect suggested this may have been one way the Romans built ships, but the suggestion was never followed up. About the same time came the discovery of the Dahshur boats, but they were considered a thing apart, the special products of an ancient people that tended to do things their own special way. In 1928 what should have been a decisive clue came to light when two huge and elaborate barges belonging to the Roman emperor Caligula were rescued from the waters of Lake Nemi some twenty miles south-east of Rome; 104–5
they had sunk there in antiquity and were resting on the bottom. They came up with the hulls from the deck down virtually intact, and these revealed the same construction as in the remains from Marseilles, though executed with much finer workmanship. They too were considered exceptional, the sort of work that the purse of an emperor could command, and a spendthrift emperor at that. But they were not at all exceptional. This was the way Greek and Roman and Phoenician shipwrights put together a hull, whether for an emperor's elegant barge or a fisherman's workaday craft.

We became aware of the truth of the matter only some four decades ago when, thanks to the development of a new branch of archaeology – marine archaeology – it became possible to examine the actual remains of ancient ships. In 1900, quite by accident, a crew of Greek sponge divers discovered off the island of Antikythera, which lies between Crete and the southern tip of the Peloponnese, the wreck of an ancient freighter that was carrying works of art; a campaign to recover its cargo got under way, and for a year a handful of sponge divers – the only personnel available – made repeated dives down to it and managed to salvage a good many precious items. Then, in 1907, history repeated itself off the port of Mahdia on the east coast of Tunis: sponge divers came upon an ancient wreck, again a campaign was mounted, and it went on until 1913. As before, sponge divers were pressed into service; working under great difficulties, they succeeded in raising much of the cargo; it, too, included

20 A marine archaeologist removes an amphora that was part of the cargo of a merchantman wrecked about 1350 BC off the town of Ulu Burun on the south coast of Asia Minor.

KD

21 Marine archaeologists at work on the wreck of a small merchantman of about 300 BC found off Kyrenia on the north coast of Cyprus. They have erected a grid over the remains; this will enable them to identify precisely the location of each part of the hull and of the objects found in it.

works of art, although the greater part consisted of columns and blocks of marble for some building. Although both projects yielded unique and invaluable material, the kind of archaeological investigation they represented had no future. It involved the use of untrained personnel, it operated with no organised plan, and whatever was accomplished was at the cost of enormous effort, time and money.

Then, in the years after the Second World War, the situation changed dramatically. An apparatus that did away with the traditional clumsy and heavy diving gear had been invented as long ago as the 1860s, but it was not until 1943 that a French naval officer, Jacques-Ives Cousteau, perfected a simple and safe version. Its basic feature consisted of one to three cylindrical tanks of compressed air connected with a mouthpiece and mounted in a harness strapped on the diver's back. A big goggle that fitted over the eyes and nose and a pair of rubber flippers that slipped 20
over the feet completed the outfit. A person so equipped could stride from a beach or dive from a cliff and, once in the water, freely move about the sea bed for half an hour or more, depending on the number of tanks carried and the depth reached. It was so easy and safe that scuba diving – diving with the Self-Contained Underwater Breathing Apparatus – became a popular sport.

Shortly after 1952 scuba divers began to be recruited for searching out and examining ancient wrecks and, where possible, raising the cargo. At first those who took part were merely interested amateurs and they worked almost as haphazardly as the sponge divers had half a century earlier. As time went on they were joined by people who had training in archaeology as well as diving. These new entrants in the field devised ways of grappling with the very special problems presented by excavating under water, and thereby founded marine archaeology, which seeks to investigate submerged ancient remains as carefully and comprehensively as traditional archaeology does those on land, taking precise measurements, noting the location of all objects found, registering each one, and 21
so on.

The organised surveys of the marine archaeologists, together with the casual sightings of scuba enthusiasts, have by now located hundreds of ancient wrecks. The discoveries off Antikythera and Mahdia had nourished rosy dreams of resurrecting masses of lost Greek art from the sea. However, as we might expect, most of the merchantmen that plied the waters of the Mediterranean in antiquity were loaded not with art objects but with humble commodities, in particular grain, wine and olive oil. And most of the wrecks that have been found proved to be carrying either wine or olive oil. This is because these were transported in amphoras, big clay jars which are able to resist the effects of the movement of water and sand and hence survive. What is more, they often preserve from destruction the wood of the hull they lie over (see Chapter 9). Of the 22
wrecks discovered to date this has proved to be the case in some thirty

instances, and in all of them it turns out that the planks, as on the Marseilles hull or Caligula's barges, were joined together with mortises and tenons.

There are basically two ways to construct a wooden boat. The one we are most familiar with, since it has been in use in the West for centuries, begins with the setting up of a sturdy skeleton of keel and frames, to 23 which a skin of planks is then fastened. The other, favoured in southern Asia and some parts of northern Europe, is just the reverse: it begins with the erecting of a strong shell of planks by pinning each plank to its neighbours; a certain amount of framing is then inserted in the shell to stiffen it. In this, the so-called shell-first technique, the planks may be joined to each other in any of three ways. One, best known because it was the way used by the Vikings, by England's shipwrights up to the time of Henry VIII, and by Scandinavian boatbuilders right up to this century, produced the clinker-built boat: each plank overlaps the one below for a 110 certain distance, and pegs or nails or rivets driven through the double thickness hold them securely together. In the other two ways, the planks are set edge to edge; what differs is the means of fastening them. One we have already described, sewing them together with some sort of binding material, a way that was in use at least as early as Old Kingdom Egypt. Another was to staple or nail them together, or join them together with

22 In this wreck of the 1st century BC, found off Cape Dramont east of St-Raphaël in southern France, the cargo of amphoras stowed in levels in the hold has preserved the wood of the bottom of the hull.

23 Detail from *The Building of St Ursula's Boat* by Paolo da Venezia (1310–58), showing shipwrights building in skeleton-first fashion the boat that is to take St Ursula from Britain to Rome. This is one of the earliest representations of skeleton-first construction.

mortises and tenons, as in the Dahshur boats. This was what Greek and Roman and Phoenician shipwrights did, but in their own special way, which frequently involved such craftsmanship that the results more resemble cabinet work than carpentry. And, unlike the Egyptians, into their finely built shells they inserted a complete set of frames.

Most of the wrecks that have been investigated date from the fourth century BC onwards, and they reveal that this distinctive form of shipbuilding was then in full flower and continued to be so for a long time, until about the end of the first century AD. During this period the shipwrights set the mortise and tenon joints close together, usually no 24–5
more than four inches (10 cm) apart and often much less; indeed, in one instance the shipwright left hardly any space at all between the joints by staggering them, putting one nearer to the inboard face of the plank and the next nearer to the outboard face. They favoured big tenons, usually 26
two inches (5 cm) broad but at times up to double that, and in depth penetrating halfway into the plank. After knocking the planks together 27
and driving the joints home, they transfixed each half of the tenon, above and below the seam, with a dowel, thereby ensuring that the joint would never come apart. And after the shell had been built up, either partly or totally, they inserted a complete set of frames to stiffen it. 28

With such close-set joinery binding the seams, there was no room for

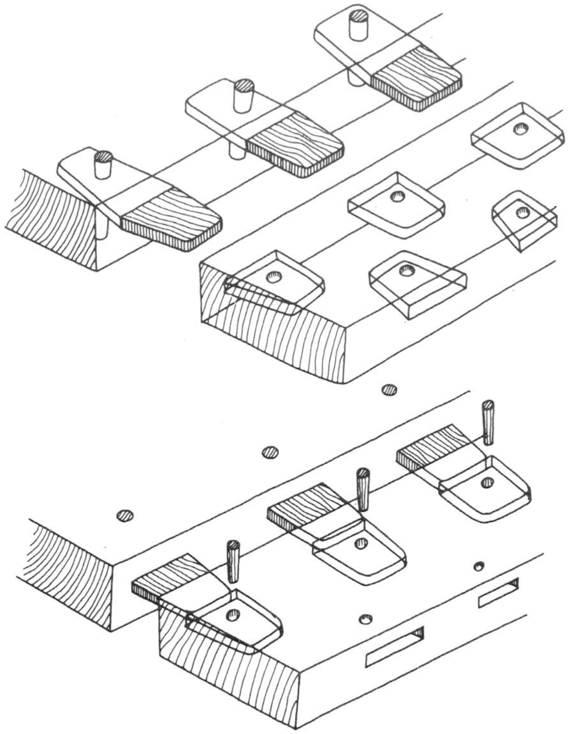

24 TOP LEFT Sketch showing the mortise and tenon joinery used in ancient shipbuilding.

25 TOP RIGHT Fragment of a plank from a wreck of about 110–80 BC found off the Grand Congloué island near Marseilles. It has been split as if filleted, laying bare the line of mortise and tenon joints in the upper and lower edges. Four mortises in the upper edge still have the tenons and transfixing dowels in place.

26 Fragment of a plank from a wreck of the early 1st century BC found off the island of Antikythera, south of Greece. The mortise and tenon joints are only $\frac{3}{8}$ inch (1 cm) apart. To reduce the danger of splitting the planks, the shipwright staggered the joints, putting them alternately nearer the outboard and inboard faces of the plank.

Colour Plate I OPPOSITE, TOP Egyptian craft, manned by seven rowers a side, in the act of towing a vessel. Note the tow-line extending from the stern. Copy of a wall painting in a tomb at Thebes, 15th century BC.

Colour Plate II Egyptian sailing craft of about 2400–2300 BC. It has a bipod mast stepped forward of amidships which carries a tall and narrow sail hung from a yard along the head and stiffened by a boom along the foot. A hand aft trims the braces; two hands in the bows, holding sounding poles, are ready to measure the depth of the water by plunging them straight down. Copy of a wall painting in a tomb at Giza.

Colour Plate III Egyptian boat used for transporting mummies. Ancient model in the British Museum. About 2000 BC.

Colour Plate IV An Egyptian noble and his family drift through the marshes in a small reed boat as he hunts birds with a throwing-stick. Wall painting from a tomb at Thebes. About 1400 BC.

27 Shipwrights adding a plank as they build up the hull of a replica of the Kyrenia wreck (see Fig. 21 and title page). The line of close-set mortise and tenon joints is clearly visible.

28 ABOVE Relief on the tombstone of a Roman shipwright, Publius Longidienus, found near Ravenna and now in the Archaeological Museum there. It shows the deceased in the act of adzing a frame to insert in the completed hull. Late 2nd or early 3rd century AD. The Latin inscription in the rectangle says, 'Longidienus pushes ahead with his work'.

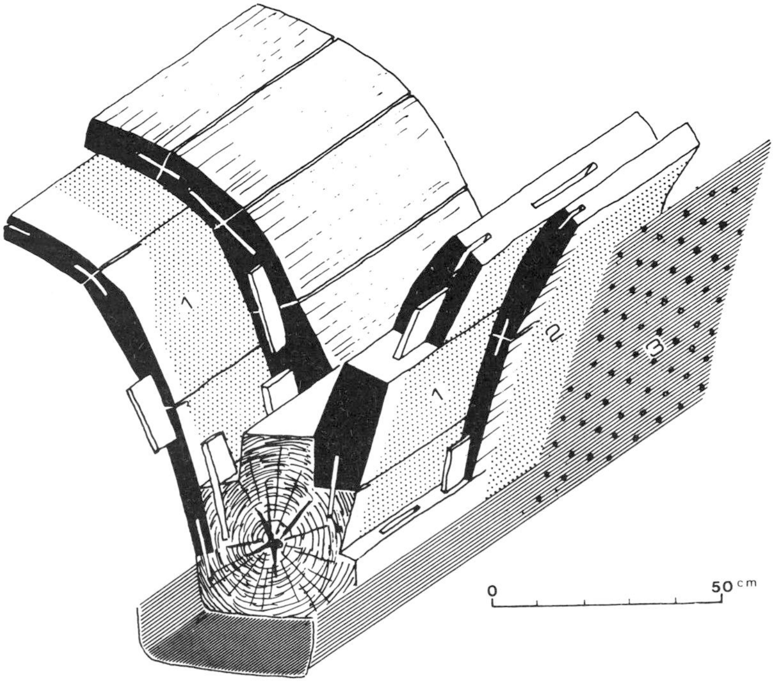

29 Sketch showing the construction of the keel and adjacent planking of a wreck of the 1st century BC found at Madrague de Giens near Toulon. It had a double layer of planking (1, 2) and was sheathed with sheets of lead laid over tarred fabric (3).

caulking, nor was there need for any: the swelling of the wood when the ship was put in the water caused the seams to close up and become watertight. On some hulls, as protection against marine borers, the underwater surface was sheathed with thin sheets of lead laid over tarred fabric and held in place by a multitude of large-headed copper tacks. 29

Once the discovery of ancient remains had revealed the special way in which the Greeks built their ships, a passage in the *Odyssey* that had long puzzled translators and commentators suddenly became clear. Homer tells how Odysseus, after losing his ship and crew in a storm, landed alone and helpless on the island of the nymph Calypso; how the nymph took him in and so enjoyed his company that she kept him there for seven years; how the gods finally forced her to let him go, and how she co-operated by providing him with the logs and tools for building himself a boat. Odysseus adzed the logs into planks, and, continues Homer, 'then bored them all and fitted them to each other. Then he hammered it [the craft] with pegs and joints.... Then he worked away setting up decks by fastening them to close-set frames.'[1] He followed, in other words, what the wrecks have revealed was standard procedure. He first 'bored them all', that is, drilled into the upper and lower edges of the planks to make the mortises (carpenters traditionally rough out mortises with the drill and then finish up with the chisel) as well as across each mortise for the transfixing pegs which would hold the tenon locked into place. Then he 'fitted them to each other', i.e., set the plank edges opposite each other to make sure each tenon was lined up with the mortise it was to go into. Then he 'hammered it with pegs and joints', i.e., knocked the planks together, driving home the tenons into the mortises and the transfixing pegs into their holes. Having built up the shell in that way, he turned to the insertion of the frames, the fastening to them of the crossbeams, and the laying on these of the deck planking.

Homer lived in the eighth century BC, and obviously this distinctive form of shipbuilding was standard practice at that time. We now know that it had been standard practice long before. In 1982 off the southern coast of Asia Minor a wreck was discovered that dates from about 1350 20
BC. Divers have removed enough of the cargo to reveal that some of the bottom planks have been preserved – and that they are fastened to each other by mortises and tenons.

The second century AD marks a turning point in ancient shipbuilding. From this time on, shipwrights gradually decreased the strength of the shell by reducing the joinery and, to compensate, increased the importance of the inserted framing. Ultimately, as we shall see later (Chapter 9), they made a transition from shell-first to skeleton-first construction.

4
The Sailing Vessel

A mighty wave, with fearful drive, broke upon
his ship and spun it about. He was hurled overboard,
the helm wrenched from his grasp. A terrifying gust
of mingled winds shattered the mast at midpoint
and swept yard and sail into the sea far off.

Odyssey 5.313–18

So Homer describes the savage storm that ultimately cast Odysseus, naked and exhausted, on the shores of the land of the Phaeacians. He was not exercising his poetic imagination; this was what one could expect when voyaging over the Aegean or eastern Mediterranean. The opening chapter in the history of the sailing vessel is the story of how a rig originally devised for the gentle waters and mild breezes of the Nile was transformed into one capable of coping with the winds and waves of the open sea.

As we have seen (Chapter 2), the first boatmen to equip their craft with sails were the Egyptians. And the first craft so equipped were galleys; the sails were to help out the efforts of a line of paddlers or, later, rowers. At some point galley crews became aware that, if they were in no hurry and could put up with the vagaries of the wind, the sail alone could do the job. They did not even have to row to get upstream, because the Nile boasts the convenience of a prevailing wind that blows opposite to its flow; all they had to do was raise sail. As a result, alongside the galley there soon came into being vessels that were moved solely by the wind.
Their rig has already been described (Chapter 2), a tall and narrow 11
squaresail that, in addition to the yard, the indispensable spar along the head, had another spar, a boom, along the foot.

About 2000 BC the dimensions of the sail were reversed: instead of being much higher than wide it became much wider than high; this was a shape better suited to handle strong winds. The change may well have been connected with the Egyptians' growing trade with the coast of the Levant to the north and the horn of Africa to the south – in other words, their seamen now had to deal more and more with the conditions to be
met on the open water. The pictures on Hatshepsut's tomb show that, at 18
least for the journey on the Red Sea, the ships were galleys whose hulls had been strengthened with trusses. But the rig is the same as that on Nile craft, a broad squaresail with a boom along the foot supported by multiple lifts.

In fact, the seagoing sailing merchantman, the type of vessel that was to dominate not only the Mediterranean but the seven seas right up to the introduction of steam, does not make its appearance in the historical record until about 1400 BC, although it was no doubt in existence somewhat earlier. A painting on the wall of an Egyptian tomb of that date at
Thebes portrays a fleet of ships arriving in a port, and the ships, no 30
question about it, are sailing vessels, for their hulls are not long and

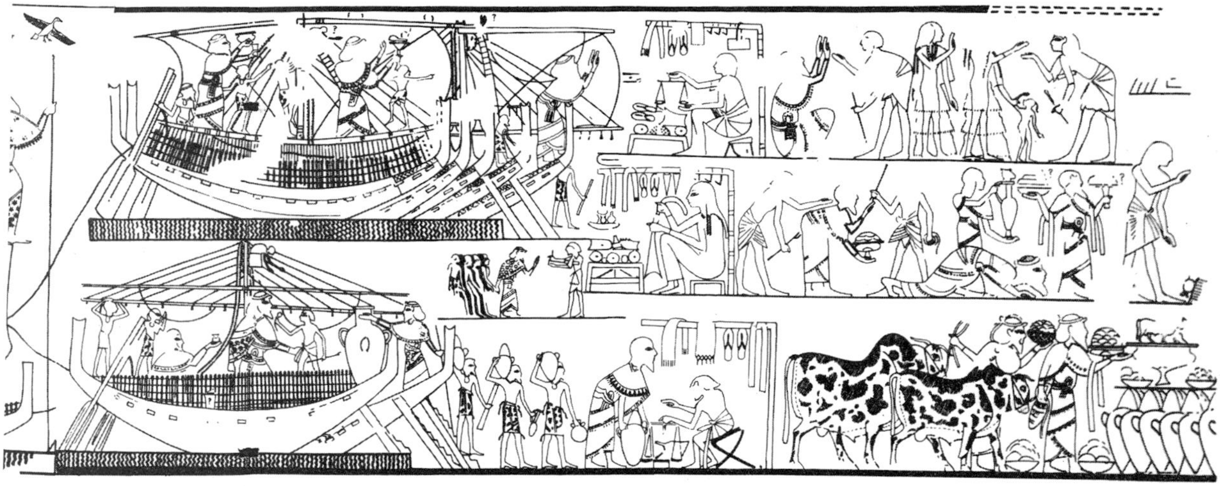

30 A fleet of Levantine merchantmen arrives at an Egyptian port. Drawing from a painting in a tomb at Thebes. About 1400 BC.

slender as on a galley but stubby and heavy, and the sides are raised by a palisade to protect cargo carried on deck; moreover, there are no indications of oars or rowers. Part of the fleet is in the process of arriving: hands have gone aloft to take in the sails, and in one vessel the skipper stands in the bows sounding with a long pole as his craft inches in toward 31
the beach. Others have already arrived. The sails have been furled, and the cargo is being unloaded down gangplanks that run from the bows to the beach (harbours were rough and ready in those days; since there were no wharves, ships were simply run in as far as possible). In front of one of the moored vessels sits an Egyptian behind a table. He must be a merchant, since a ship's officer is trying to sell him a large jar from the cargo, probably filled with wine or olive oil, for no good grade of either was produced in Egypt; behind, a line of crewmen unload still more jars. The fleet had brought in passengers as well as cargo, as a vignette in the upper right-hand corner reveals: there a ship's officer appears to be asking a favour of an Egyptian official for two women and a child who precede him; they must have come off his vessel, since their dress, with its elaborate three-tiered skirt, is distinctly un-Egyptian.

The home port of the fleet was somewhere on the Levantine coast. The depiction of the crews puts this beyond doubt: they are Semites, for, totally unlike the beardless, snub-nosed Egyptians who dress in loin cloths, they have beards and hooked profiles and the officers wear gaily embroidered ankle-length robes. The ships are more strongly built than contemporary Egyptian craft, which, as we have seen, when venturing on open water needed a truss to add support to bow and stern; those pictured here lack that feature. On the other hand, they are rigged in Egyptian fashion: each has a single broad squaresail stretched along the foot by a boom which is supported by multiple lifts. Apparently, the sailors of the Levantine coast, although they fashioned their own kind of hull, sturdier than the Egyptian, borrowed the Egyptian rig.

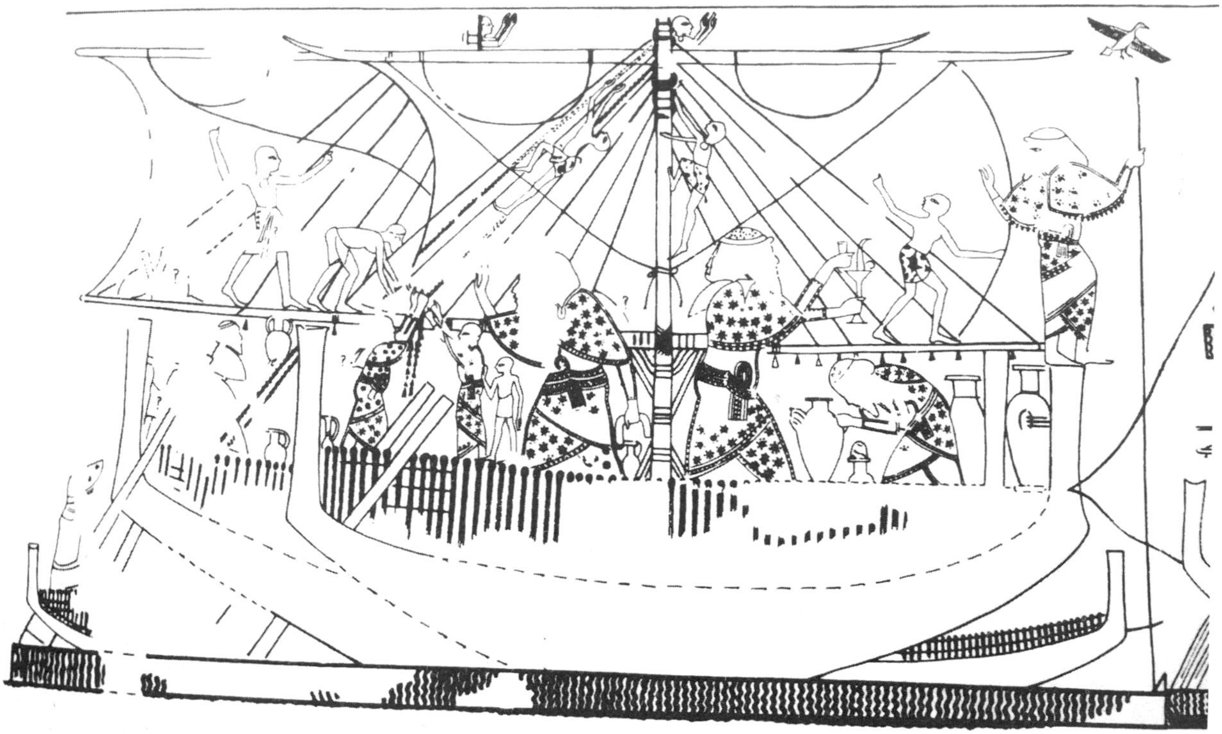

31 A Levantine merchantman approaches port. The skipper, in elaborate dress, stands in the bows, sounding the depth with a long pole. Two men in equally elaborate dress, probably the merchants who own the cargo, are amidships; one holds a cup, presumably for a libation to celebrate their safe arrival. The other figures more or less elaborately dressed are the ship's officers; the deckhands wear loincloths.

As it happens, they were not the only ones: thanks to recent archaeological discoveries, we now know that it found favour in the Aegean as well as along the Levant. Some seventy-five miles north of Crete lies Santorini – or Thera, to give it its ancient name – a small island with a large and vigorous volcano. Here a prosperous town flourished until, about 1600 BC, the volcano erupted mightily and covered the town under a blanket of ash that in places was over 100 feet (30 m) thick. Excavation of the site was undertaken in 1967, and soon the archaeologists' spades began to lay bare the remains of handsome houses whose walls were decorated with elaborate paintings. One room boasted a frieze depicting a naval procession, thereby furnishing us with the only surviving detailed representations of ships of this period. Six long slender galleys are being 32
paddled along a coast; in the waters about them are small craft of various kinds. That they are being paddled and not rowed is curious; except for canoes or the like, paddles had been supplanted by oars almost a millennium earlier. The best explanation is that they are taking part in some traditional ceremony in which the age-old way of doing things was maintained, like the use of horse-drawn carriages today at coronations, certain funerals and similar occasions.

The sails on the galleys are furled, but it is clear that they have that typical Egyptian feature, a boom along the foot. Only one ship in the picture has sail raised, a small craft that is not part of the procession. It is very badly preserved but enough of the original paint survives to show that the sail was of Egyptian type: it has the tell-tale boom. In borrowing such a sail, Aegean and Levantine seamen did themselves no great service; it was ill-suited for use on the open sea. The problem was the boom: because of it, there was no way to shorten sail. For boatmen on the Nile this was not serious; at the sight of an oncoming storm, they could head for the nearest bank. But for seamen on the Aegean or eastern Mediterranean, where quick refuge could not be counted on, it was very serious. And they shortly did something about it.

In Chapter 2 we dealt with the reliefs illustrating the battle fought in 1190 BC in which Pharaoh Ramses III repulsed an attempt to invade Egypt by land and sea. The pictures, we noted, reveal that a fundamental change had taken place in the way the Egyptians built their ships. They reveal as well a fundamental change in the way Egyptians rigged their ships. On both the Egyptian and the enemy craft the sails no longer have a boom; they are loose-footed. What is more, the artist portrays them as furled by means of lines that run from evenly spaced points along the yard down to the deck. These are brails, a system of lines that provides, as we shall see in a moment, an easy and rapid way to shorten sail. This rig, a loose-footed squaresail with brails, was to be the rig *par excellence* of the ancient world for the next two millennia, right up to its close. Since Egypt's enemies had sailed down the eastern Mediterrarean to make their attack, we may presume that their ships bore such a rig because it was standard for those waters. And since the seamen of those waters were the ones with the greatest need for it, we may further presume that they were its creators and that the Egyptians had borrowed it. 19

The attack on Egypt in 1190 BC was part of a large-scale movement

32 Minoan galleys driven by a line of paddlers. The use of so outdated a means of propulsion may indicate that they are taking part in some ceremonial procession. Wall painting from Thera, now in the National Archaeological Museum, Athens. About 1600 BC.

of aggressive peoples that swept over the lands around the Aegean and eastern Mediterranean. It brought to an end many of the states that were flourishing at the time and inaugurated what is often referred to as a dark age, two or three centuries when the level of civilisation in the area remained at low ebb. About 900 BC the darkness recedes, and there opens the best-known period of ancient history, the long span of time that was dominated first by the Greeks and then by the Romans.

From about 900 to 500 BC, two major maritime peoples shared the Aegean and eastern Mediterranean, the Phoenicians and the Greeks. Commerce burgeoned, and both peoples devised their own kind of merchantmen to take part in it.

The Phoenicians went in for hulls that were broad of beam and rounded at both stem and stern, and usually garnished with a horse's head as adornment for the prow. Greek writers dubbed such craft either *gauloi* ('tubs') because of their shape or *hippoi* ('horses') because of the figurehead. We have but a single representation of a sailing ship of this
34 type, and that happens to be on a Hebrew seal of the eighth or seventh century BC; obviously the type had been borrowed by some of the Phoenicians' neighbours. Since the artist had so little space to work with, there is scant detail; of the lines of the rigging, for example, he has included only the forestays and backstays. In rendering the sail he has made the line along the bottom as heavy as that along the top. This would seem to indicate that it had a boom; in other words, there were still sailing craft that clung to the traditional Egyptian rig. It was not yet totally obsolete.

However, by the beginning of the sixth century BC, it most certainly was. All representations, whether of warships or merchantmen, whether
33 of Phoenician or Greek craft, show only the broad loose-footed squaresail

33 OPPOSITE Phoenician warships and transports. The warships carry loose-footed square sails. Drawn from a relief in the palace of Sennacherib (704–681 BC) at Nineveh.

34 Sailing vessel depicted on a Hebrew seal of the 8th–7th century BC. Private collection.

35 OVERLEAF Greek war galleys under sail. Brails running at intervals from the foot up the forward surface to the yard and then over the yard down to the deck aft permit shortening and furling of the sail. Horizontal lines across the forward surface strengthen the canvas. Painting on an Athenian cup in the Louvre, Paris. Second half of the 6th century BC.

fitted with brails. The pictures by Greek artists, executed with great skill, are particularly illuminating. The yard, in order to span so wide a sail, is generally made, as on Hatshepsut's ships, of two tapering spars tied
35 together at their thick ends. To each yard-arm is fastened a brace to move the sail laterally, and to each of the lower corners a sheet to trim the sail in or let it belly out. The brails, spaced at regular intervals, run from the foot of the sail up the forward surface to the yard; they pass over the yard
V guided by fairleads and then continue down to the deck aft. They permit total control of the sail. By pulling on all the brails at once, hands were able to bunch it up toward the yard, the way a venetian blind is raised, and leave exposed just the proper expanse that the strength of the wind
VI called for. To furl sail they simply pulled the brails all the way up. By pulling on only certain of the brails, they could offer a triangular expanse, when that was appropriate. In short, brails provided a flexible, simple and rapid way to shorten sail, much superior to the reef-points that replaced them in the Middle Ages and remained in use until the last days of wind-driven merchantmen.

The brails, as just noted, traversed vertically the forward surface of the
35 sail. In this age there was added a set of lines that traversed it horizontally to form, along with the brails, a complete network. The purpose was to reinforce the material of which the sail was made: the mesh of lines kept it from tearing when struck by violent gusts of wind.

An especially fine representation of a Greek merchantman appears on a cup that dates from about 510 BC. The artist portrays the vessel at two successive moments and, in so doing, reveals how useful a piece of
36 equipment the brails were. In the first scene the vessel is bowling along before a wind that must be very strong because the sail is brailed up all along its width, leaving only a triangular patch of canvas near each yard-arm to draw. The skipper is unaware that a pirate galley is in full chase
37 under oars and sail. In the second scene he has perceived the danger: despite the strength of the wind, he has loosed all the brails and is flying along with every inch of canvas drawing. On the galley, since it is now within attacking range, the commander is doing just the opposite: he is having his crew haul on the brails in order to furl the sail preparatory to coming alongside his prey and boarding. The shortening or letting out of sail involved merely pulling on or slacking off lines, not tying and untying knots as later ages would have to do.

The merchantman pictured is a handsome craft with a capacious hull and a concave prow reminiscent of the prows on clipper ships. Stem and stern end simply, without figureheads. It carries landing ladders in two lengths, long and short; it was prepared, in other words, to load or unload off beaches where the water was either shallow or deep.

A painting on the wall of an Etruscan tomb dating from some thirty
38 years later reveals the next major step in the development of the ancient sailing vessel. It shows a merchantman with a hull shaped very much like

36 A pirate galley under full sail pursues a Greek merchantman whose skipper, unaware of the danger, has partially brailed up his sail to shorten it, since a strong wind is blowing. Painting on an Athenian cup in the British Museum. Late 6th century BC.

37 Hands on the galley seize the brails to furl sail preparatory to boarding the merchantman, whose skipper, now aware of the danger, has let out the brails and is travelling under full canvas in an effort to escape capture.

38 Etruscan merchantman rigged with a foresail. The foremast has a forward rake, a feature that continues through the centuries. Drawing from a painting in a tomb at Tarquinia, Italy. Early 5th century BC.

that of the vessel on the cup and the same sort of mainsail. However, this ship is a two-master: it has a foresail, a slightly smaller version of the mainsail set on a mast with a distinct rake forward that is stepped on the foredeck. This, the *artemon* as the Greeks called it, from now on will be a standard feature of seagoing merchantmen.

We have reached the opening decades of the fifth century BC. They mark the beginning of Greece's celebrated Classical Age, an age that was marked in the naval sphere by the appearance of a new version of the war galley. Let us turn back to trace its development.

5

The Warship: Origin and Early Development

The recorded history of the ancient Near East begins in the third millennium BC. During the ensuing centuries there was no lack of fighting, but none took place on the sea. The cities of Babylonia battled with each other, the rulers of Akkad extended their conquests into what is today Syria and Iraq, the pharaohs' soldiers marched into Sinai and the lower part of Palestine to subjugate the local populations, but the clashes were all on land. That state of affairs changed in the next millennium. By its end the sea had begun to assume the role it was to play throughout the ages, and the fundamental instrument of naval combat, the warship, had come into being.

To trace its history we must go back to the early third millennium BC when the galley first appears, a long and slender vessel driven by a line of rowers on each side (Chapter 2). As time passed, two general types emerged. One, designed to transport goods and passengers without having to depend totally on the wind as sailing vessels did, was made wide and heavy in order to provide room for cargo and the strength to carry it. Such craft – merchant galleys, as we may call them – were rarely in a hurry; they proceeded for the most part under sail and resorted to their oars only when there was no wind, or it was too feeble, or it came from the wrong direction. Galleys of the second type were designed to transport dispatches or important personnel as expeditiously as possible. Consequently they were usually in a hurry, and so were made light and slender. Sail was raised whenever the wind supplied sufficient drive; the moment it fell below that, out came the oars. This was the type that developed into the man-of-war.

What records have survived indicate that the first role ships played in warfare was as transports. The earliest instance dates from around 2300 BC; it occurred during one of the forays that Egypt was continually making into Palestine. An inscription has been found at Abydos that gives the life story of Uni, the Egyptian commander of the expedition. Among the achievements he lists is that he 'crossed over in transports with these troops [i.e., those the pharaoh had placed under his command]' and 'made a landing at the rear of the heights of the mountain range in the north of the land.'[1] The heights referred to are most probably Mt Carmel, where Haifa now stands, close to 200 nautical miles from the nearest point of the delta of the Nile. He surely used galleys and not sailing ships, since the men had to arrive on time and the northerly winds that prevail in the area would not have been favourable. And he surely stayed close to the coast with stops *en route* to feed and rest the men, since loaded galleys had scant space for amenities.

By the time of Thutmose III (1504–1450 BC), such transport of troops was no unusual procedure. For two decades Thutmose led his armies almost yearly into Palestine, Phoenicia, Syria and beyond, and from his fifth campaign onwards he brought at least part of his forces by sea, disembarking them at harbours on the Phoenician coast which he foresightedly provisioned with supplies of food. The men not only arrived more quickly but were in better shape than those who went by land, having been spared a long and exhausting march.

Either type of galley, the heavy and slow or the fast and light, could have been used on these occasions, since the ships were serving only as carriers. The crucial step that transformed the galley into a man-of-war was reserved for the light, fast type. It already had the speed and manoeuvrability that combat required. What it needed was armament, and this was provided by adding to the crew a number of men-at-arms – in other words, a contingent of marines.

Thutmose, in the report of his military triumphs that he had inscribed on the walls of a temple at Karnak, notes that, during the return from his fifth campaign in the Levant, probably around 1475 BC, 'there was a seizing of two ships ... loaded with everything, with male and female slaves, copper, lead, emery, and every good thing.'[2] This is the first act of piracy on record. Apparently the fleet of transports ran across a pair of tempting prizes, and Thutmose ordered some of his galleys, no doubt of the fast type, to give chase. If they were from among the transports, the soldiers aboard could have effected the capture. But it is quite possible that his aggregation included some fighting ships manned with marine units, and it was these he sent in pursuit. In any event, by the next century such warcraft were certainly in existence, for attacks were taking place that imply their use. Around 1375 BC, for example, Rib-Addi, the ruler of Byblos (located some twenty-five miles north of modern Beirut), a port theoretically under Egypt's protection at the time, writes in a letter to the pharaoh that '[the enemy] has seized one of my ships and has actually sailed forth on the sea to capture my other ships.'[3] These foes of his were even able to establish a blockade, for a letter from an allied ruler wails that '[the enemy] has placed ships ... so that grain cannot be brought into Simyra [just north of Byblos]. We cannot enter Simyra.'[4] The ships placed so as to ban entrance to Simyra could only have been hostile warcraft, fast galleys carrying ample numbers of fighting men.

In addition to piracy and blockade such as Rib-Addi complains of, much raiding of coastal settlements went on during the latter half of the second millennium BC. This called for a crew of a different make-up. There were no marines, or very few. Instead the benches were manned by rowers who could double as men-at-arms. They went aboard clutching shield, spear and sword, which they stored out of the way. Taking their places at the oars, they plied them until the site to be attacked was reached; here they dropped their oars and picked up their weapons. The galleys that Agamemnon, Odysseus, Achilles and the rest of Homer's heroes commanded in their famed war against Troy were all manned in this way. Two thousand years later, the Vikings manned theirs in the same way for their attacks on the coasts of Britain, northern Europe and elsewhere.

Colour Plate V Fore part of a Greek galley under sail: the fairleads that guide the brails over the yard are clearly visible. The figure standing on the prow seems to be undergoing the ancient equivalent of walking the plank. Painting on an Athenian jug in the British Museum. Late 6th century BC.

Colour Plate VI Odysseus' ship passing the Sirens. Odysseus stuffed the crew's ears with wax to block out the Sirens' irresistible song, but did not stuff his own; he wanted to hear it but without the risk of being enticed to his destruction, so he had himself lashed securely to the mast. The sail has been brailed up to the yard and the vessel proceeds under oars alone. Painting on an Athenian jar in the British Museum. Late 6th to early 5th century BC.

Colour Plate VII Decked two-level war galley. The marine contingent, consisting of three archers (two near the prow, one near the stern) and three spearsmen, fight from the deck. Scene on an Etruscan jug in the British Museum. About 500 BC.

39 Fragment of a painting of Minoan galleys in battle. A marine stands on the foredeck of one ship, grasping a lance. Alongside is the fore part of another vessel, whose slender prow ornament has been bent, presumably the result of battle damage. Falling into, or swimming in, the water are men from some disabled ship. Wall painting from Thera, now in the National Archaeological Museum, Athens. About 1600 BC.

But galleys driven by warrior-oarsmen were for raiding parties, not for clashes with enemy craft. For this units of marines were essential, men whose sole duty was to fight. They were mostly archers and javelineers. A naval battle began when the galleys of hostile fleets came within bowshot. It was just like a battle on land, save that the combatants fired their arrows or hurled their javelins from an unsteady ship's floor or deck instead of solid ground. As the opposing vessels neared each other, grapnels were heaved to hold them in close embrace, the marines thrust with spears and slashed with swords as well as discharged missiles, and victory went to the commander whose men were able to storm across and defeat those arrayed against them. We have several times referred (Chapters 2, 4) to the great relief commissioned by Ramses III to commemorate the decisive battle in 1190 BC in which his ships destroyed 19
an enemy fleet at the mouth of the Nile. It illustrates graphically what naval actions of the age looked like. The relief also reveals that the warcraft of different navies, though all basically of the same type – multi-oared galleys with complements of marines – could vary considerably in appearance.

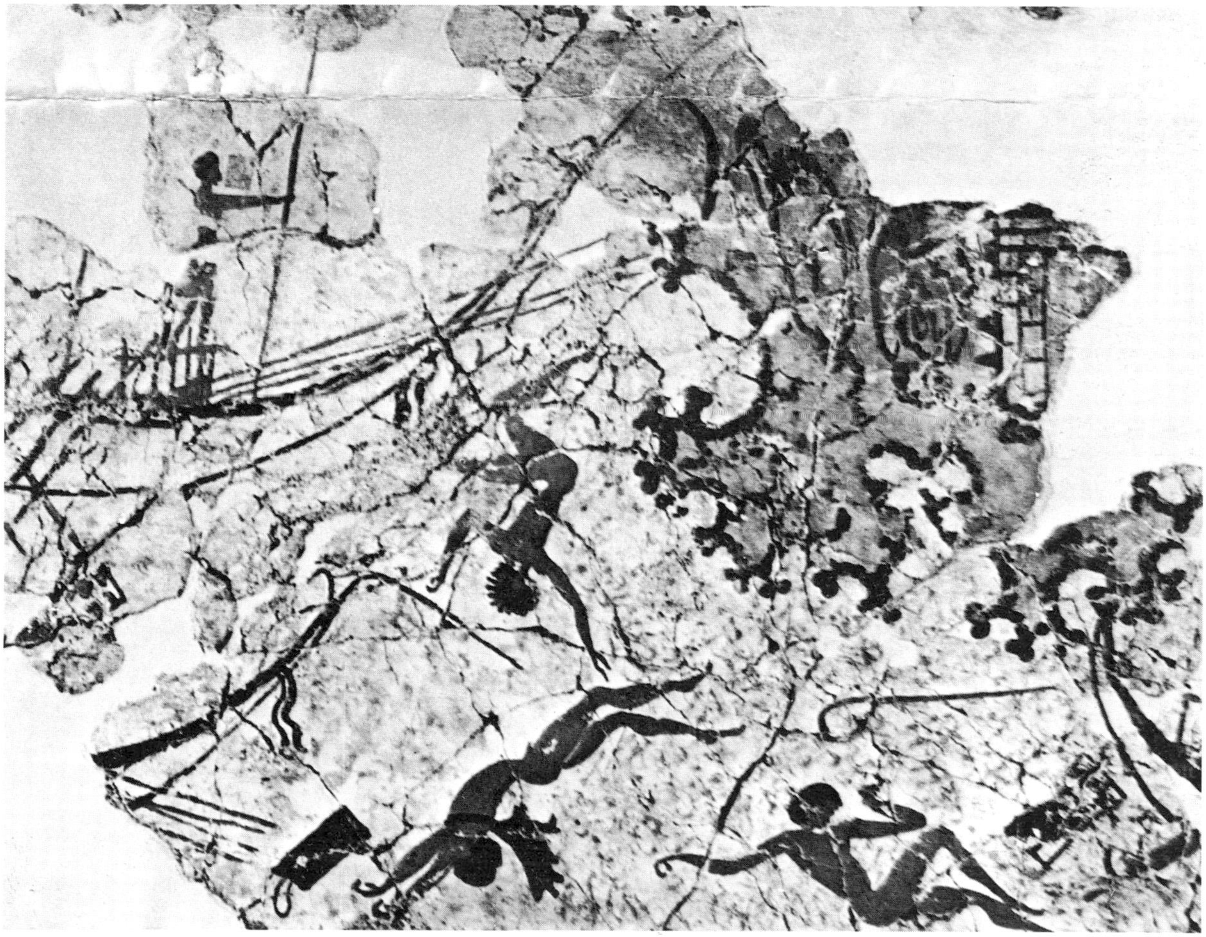

The earliest surviving detailed representations of warships are furnished by the wall-paintings of about 1600 BC from Thera, which we had
occasion to mention in the previous chapter. One scene portrays a line 32
of elegant elongated galleys in a ceremonial procession, while another
scene, unfortunately very fragmentary, shows one such vessel in action; 39
a marine grasping a long spear stands at the ready on the foredeck. The ships are open craft save for some decking at prow and stern (completely decked galleys were not to appear until over a millennium later). Aft the hull ends in a low curved sternpost decorated with elaborate carving; forward it ends in a slender stempost that curves up high and tapers to a point. The vessels are shown with masts retracted and sails tightly furled, but it is clear that the rig, like that of contemporary Egyptian craft (Chapter 2), is a broad squaresail with its foot stiffened by a boom.

Ramses' relief, dating from four centuries later, depicts warships of
two types, the Egyptians' and the invaders', both very different from the 19
type in the Thera paintings. They share some features with each other. Both are open galleys with decking only at prow and stern. Both are rigged in the same way, with a broad loose-footed squaresail. Thereafter they part company. As we noted earlier, the Egyptian craft have a hull that curves up aft into a low, plain sternpost but lacks a stempost; the forward end comes to a blunt point carved in the shape of a lion's head. A bulwark running along the side shields the rowers. The invaders' craft have a hull that is much less curved and at the ends angles sharply upward into a tall vertical stempost and sternpost. They are shown without rowers, but that does not mean they are sailing vessels. In the inscription accompanying the relief Ramses boasts of how the enemy ships that 'entered the river-mouths [of the Nile] were like birds ensnared in the net';[5] presumably he had set a trap and caught them unawares while at anchor with the oars secured.

The invaders pictured in Ramses' relief, as we have already pointed out (Chapter 4), were part of a wave of aggressive peoples who swept over the Mediterranean at this time and brought in their wake political and economic turmoil. By about 900 BC stability returns, and new players make their debut on the maritime stage, notably the Phoenician city-states on the Levantine coast, such as Tyre and Sidon, and the Greek city-states along the coast of the mainland and on the Aegean islands, such as Athens, Corinth, Miletus. And the war galleys of all have a new feature that must have revolutionised combat on the sea as radically as would the introduction of naval guns some 2000 years later. From the prow there protrudes at the waterline a massive elongation that ends in a point and is encased in bronze sheathing – a ram, as it is called from its similarity in function to the battering ram of siege warfare: just as a battering ram was thrust forward by a crew of soldiers to smash in an enemy gate or wall, so a ship's ram was thrust forward by the crew of rowers to smash in an enemy hull.

The introduction of the ram brought about a transformation in naval warfare. Hitherto the war galley had been little more than a fast transport whose prime purpose was to ferry marines close enough to fight it out. That form of combat still went on, indeed would go on until the demise of the oared warship. But now there was another, equally important, form. Galleys were now equipped to turn themselves into self-propelled projectiles: they could disable or destroy an enemy vessel by driving the point of the ram into its hull.

The ram affected naval logistics as radically as naval combat. Hitherto any galley, so long as it was reasonably sturdy and fast, could be pressed into use as a warship; now only galleys with rams were suitable. And such galleys had to be built in a very special way to sustain the shock of ramming, while the protruding snout had to be encased in bronze to keep it from shattering. As a result, building a navy took far more money than it had before: not only was there the cost of expensive raw materials – appropriately heavy timbers, hundreds of pounds of bronze – but also of skilled labour, carpenters adept in fashioning the new kind of prow and metalworkers in fashioning the casing. Only the wealthy among the Greek and Phoenician city-states could now afford a navy.

We are able to follow the emergence and development of the new weapon thanks in particular to a liking that Greek artists of this period had for decorating objects, from jewellery to kitchenware, with representations of warships. The earliest example of a galley with a ram, an engraving on the catch-plate of a bronze fibula (ornamental safety-pin) 40
found at Athens, dates from about 850 BC; since galleys without the ram are pictured down to about 1150 BC, the invention must have taken place during the intervening centuries. Then follows a series of pictures on Greek vases dating from 850 to about 700 BC, all showing war galleys 41–3
with the ram. And a relief from the palace of the Assyrian king Sennacherib, who ruled from 704 to 681 BC, adds a representation of a Phoenician warship and supplies a significant detail: a pair of vertical 47
lines toward the after end of the projection indicates where the bronze casing ended.

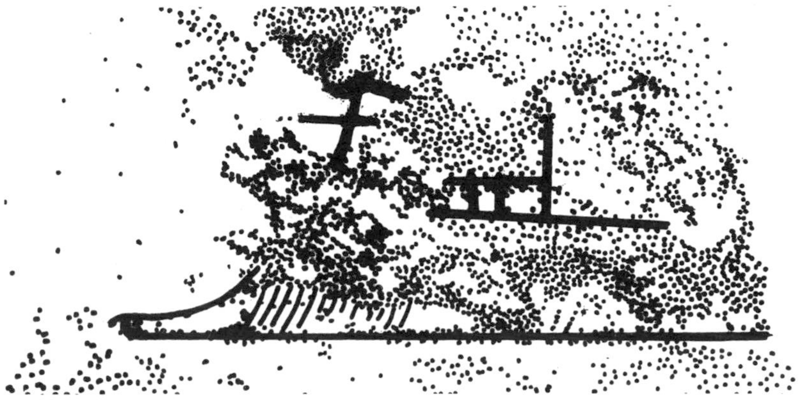

40 The earliest representation of a war galley with a ram. From an engraving on a bronze fibula found at Athens. About 850 BC.

41 ABOVE A Greek war galley under attack on a beach. Swordsmen and archers standing on a deck that runs along the centreline fight off the enemy. Painting on a bowl in the Metropolitan Museum of Art, New York. First half of the 8th century BC.

42 LEFT A Greek war galley cruising. The rowers ply their oars from the level of the raised deck. Painting on a bowl in the Louvre, Paris. Mid-8th century BC.

The pictures reveal as well what steps were taken to meet the strenuous new demands that the introduction of the ram made on a galley's hull and crew.

First, the hull. In the representations the ram is consistently shown springing from a massive base; obviously the whole prow area was powerfully reinforced to withstand the effect of a deliberately provoked violent collision. And some galleys were now given a deck that ran from 41–2
stem to stern along the centreline, leaving open space along the side where the rowers sat. As protection for these, the sides of the vessel were raised above their heads, at first by some sort of latticework and then more solidly so that the rowers appear to ply their oars framed in 43
rectangular openings. The addition of the deck along the centre of the ship and the building up of the sides supplemented the reinforcement of the prow area by stiffening the rest of the hull. Though low open galleys fitted with the ram remained in use, it was the heavier high-sided and partially decked galley that was to become the warship proper.

Next, the crew. The more rowers a galley had, the harder a stroke of the ram it could deliver. In the *Iliad* and the *Odyssey* the sizes of galley that Homer mentions most frequently are the twenty-oared and the fifty-oared. The pictures of this period show varying numbers, from eight to nineteen rowers a side, but we cannot expect photographic reproduction from painters of pottery. Vessels with eight to a side may well stand for the twenty-oared type, those with nineteen for the fifty-oared. It was the fifty-oared that proved to be the most desirable size for combat, for, down to about 550 BC or so, it was the ship of the line in Greek navies. This emerges from the Greek historians' accounts of the period: the technical term they use there for the galley that plays the key role in naval warfare is *pentekontoros* (penteconter, as it is usually transcribed), which 49
means literally 'fifty-er'. The accounts furnish no details, but we can at least make a guess as to how long the ship was. We must allow 3 feet for each oarsman, so twenty-five on a side would have required 75 feet, and we may add 40 or 50 more for foredeck, afterdeck and ram; a penteconter then would have been in the neighbourhood of 125 feet (38 m) in length. Another type of galley that turns up frequently in the naval history of the period is the triaconter (*triakonteres*), 'thirty-er', that is, with fifteen 50

43 RIGHT Greek war galleys rowed by two levels of oarsmen, one at gunwale level and the other at raised deck level. Fragments of pottery found at Athens. Late 8th century BC.

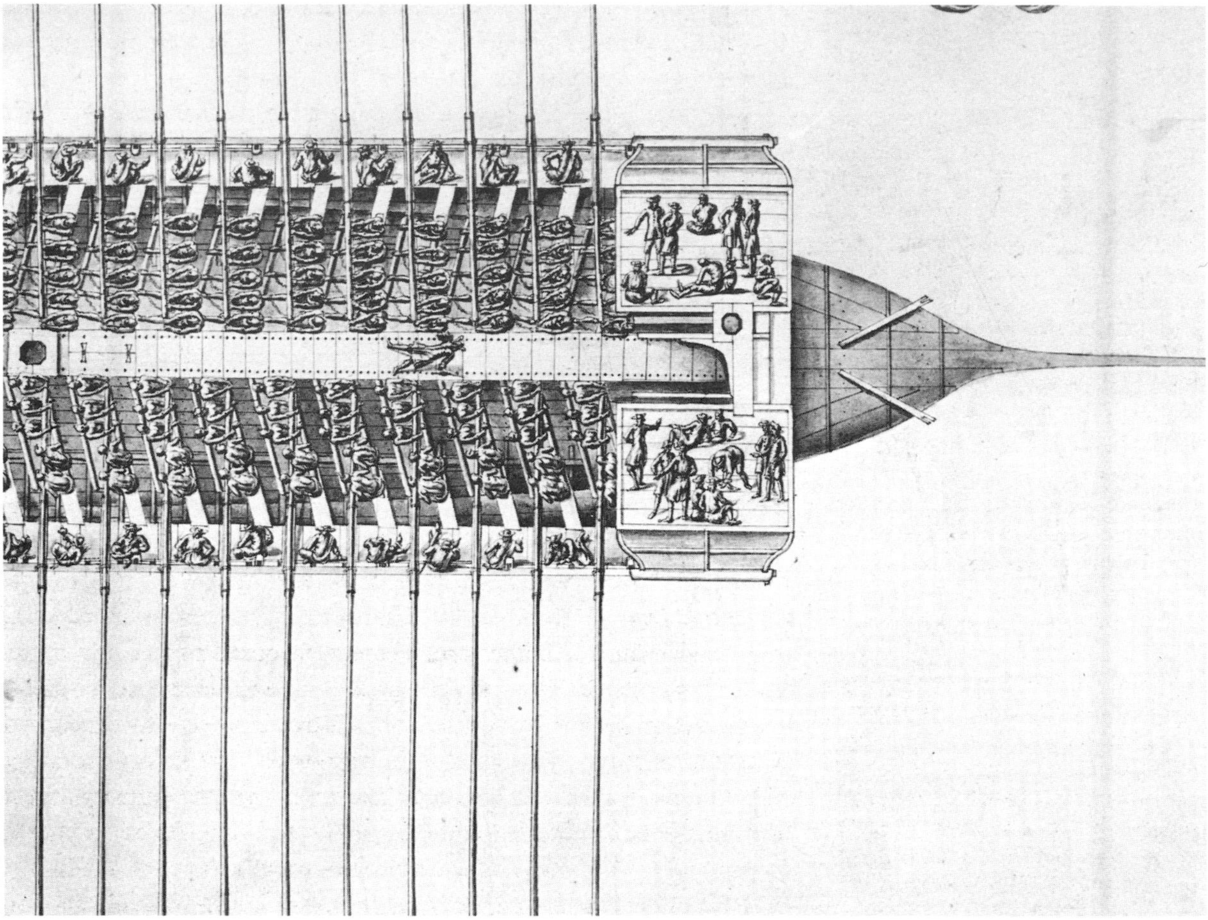

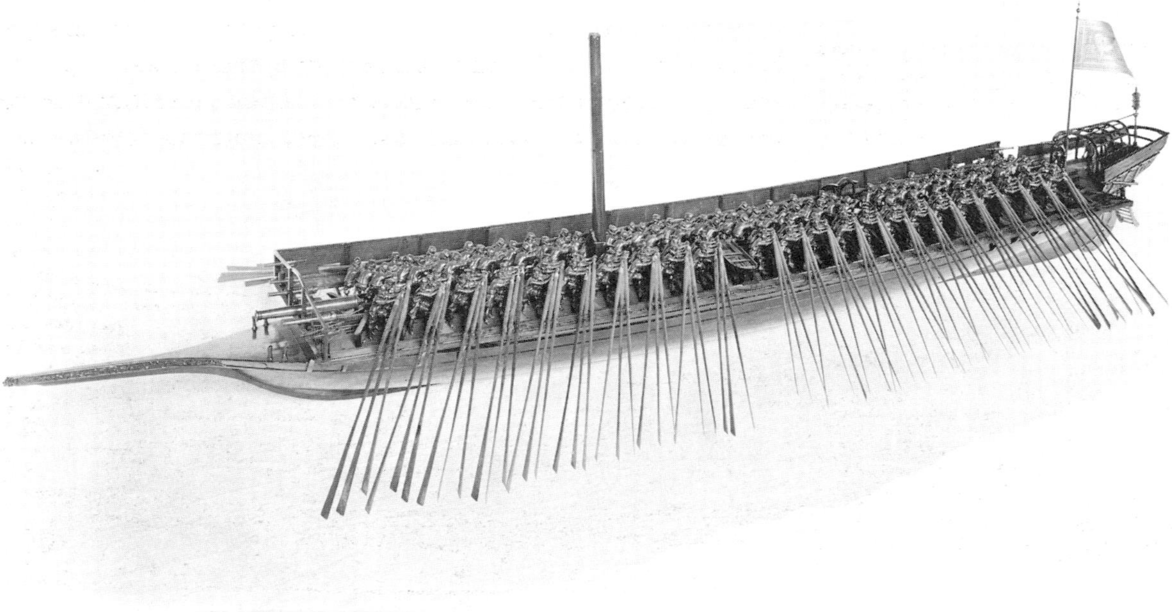

rowers a side; this would have been in the neighbourhood of 75 feet (23 m) in length. All indications are that both types were very narrow, with a length to beam ratio of perhaps 10 to 1.

The more drive a galley boasted, the more efficient a weapon it was. The only way to provide more drive was by fitting in more rowers. But, in a penteconter, with twenty-five men seated in an extended line, adding more to that line would make the hull dangerously long, would at the very least sap its strength – and strength was as important as drive for vessels that had to engage in the bruising style of combat ramming entailed. How was it possible to increase the number of rowers without increasing the length of the hull too much and thereby enfeebling it?

The history of oared warships reveals a number of ways in which naval architects met the problem. In the galleys most of us are familiar with, the notorious slave-driven units of the Mediterranean navies of the sixteenth to the eighteenth centuries, their solution was to replace one-man oars with long sweeps pulled by a line of men, usually three or four. 44
This provided an enormous increase in muscle without any in the length of the hull (though there was necessarily an increase in beam, resulting in a heavier ship). Another arrangement, favoured particularly by the Venetian navy in the fifteenth century, was to keep the one-man oars but to group them in clusters of three or four with the rowers seated alongside 45
each other on the same bench. The power was thus trebled or quadrupled without a proportionate increase in the vessel's length. Although pulled by only one man each, the oars had to be very long, almost as long as the multiple-rower sweeps, and such oars cannot be operated from a seated position; the rowers must rise from the bench to a full standing position to dip the blade and then throw themselves back on the bench to drive it through the water.

Yet another solution to the problem was to put the oarsmen in superimposed levels instead of all on the same level, and this was the way the ancient naval architects chose to go. A great advantage was that it allowed the use of short one-man oars; the rowers could pull from a seated

44 LEFT A French galley of the 18th century driven by five-man sweeps. The ship is portrayed in the act of turning round. The port rowers are pulling ahead. To ply such long oars the men cannot remain seated but must rise to a standing position to deliver the stroke; in this case they have risen from the bench and placed their chained foot on a step in front of the bench in order to gain even greater height. The starboard oars are backing water. The two men nearest the rail push from the bench while the three others have slipped round to the after side of the oar to get their backs into the pull; since there are no hand-holds on this side, they must grasp the oar as best they can. From a manuscript in the Bibliothèque du Service Hydrographique, Paris (no. 1489, fig. 22).

45 BELOW LEFT A Venetian galley of the 15th-16th century. There is one man to each oar, and the oars are grouped in clusters of three with the three rowers seated on the same bench. Since this requires oars of great length, the men must rise from the bench to deliver the stroke just as in galleys with multi-rower sweeps. Modern model in the Museo Storico Navale, Venice.

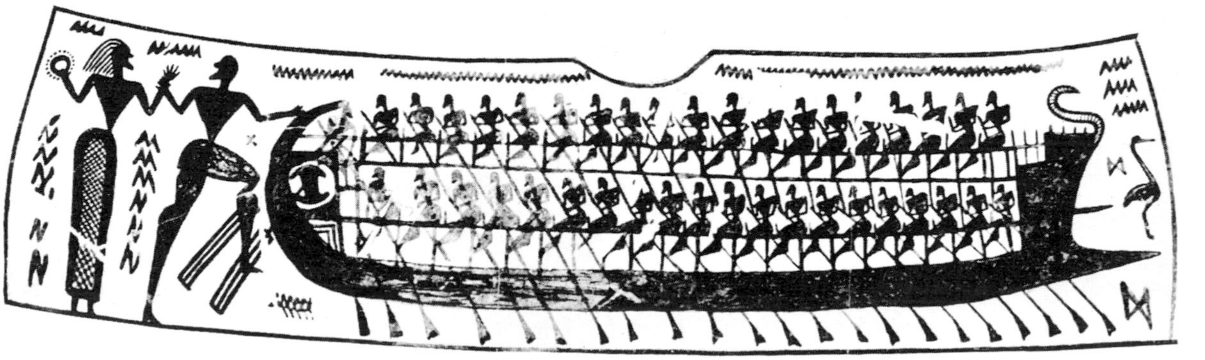

46 BELOW An early two-level Greek war galley. Painting on a bowl from Thebes, now in the British Museum. Second half of the 8th century BC.

47 Phoenician two-level war galley. The men on the lower level, seated inside the hull, work the oars through ports in the side. Those on the upper level row from the gunwale. Relief from the palace of Sennacherib (704–681 BC) at Nineveh, now in the British Museum.

position as they always had. Sometime in the eighth century BC galleys
were launched whose rowers were split into two banks, an upper and a
lower. In the case of the penteconter this made possible a hull that was
shorter than the single-level version by over a third, was sturdier and
more seaworthy, and offered a good deal less of a target to enemy rams.
46 In the earliest examples of the two-level galley, the lower bank rows from
the traditional place, the gunwale, and the upper from the height of the
deck. By 700 BC, as the relief from Sennacherib's palace reveals, the naval
47 architects had improved matters considerably by designing a compact
galley with a deepened hull in which the upper bank rows from the
gunwale and the lower through ports cut in the side. To fit everybody in
with economical use of space, the oars of the two levels are staggered:
each one of the upper is centred over the space between two of the lower.

The century from 600 to 500 BC is particularly well documented, since
warships were among the favourite motifs of the decorators of Greek
black-figured pottery (so called because the figures were painted black
and the background left the natural colour of the clay). They particularly
liked to paint them along the inside of the rim of *kraters*, the large bowls
the Greeks used for mixing wine and water (it was customary to drink
wine in this diluted fashion; only alcoholics took it neat), so that, when
the bowl was filled up to the rim, the vessels gave the illusion of sailing
upon the surface of the contents. The illustrations portray galleys of
48–9 varied makes – undecked galleys both one-level and two-level, decked
50, VII galleys both one-level and two-level – and of various sizes: twenty-oared,
triaconters, penteconters. The single-level galleys, elegantly long and
slender, are veritable seagoing greyhounds.

The pictures of this century reveal a significant change in the shape of
49, VII the ram: it no longer ends in a point but in a blunt face; often the whole
48, 50 prolongation is fashioned to resemble a boar's head with its snub nose
forming the front face. Very likely this was the result of combat experience. The ram ending in a point disabled an enemy by punching a hole in the hull, but ran the risk of getting wedged in the hole; if this happened and the attacking vessel could not quickly prise itself free, it became a helpless target for any hostile craft nearby. The blunt-faced ram avoided such danger by delivering a pounding blow that, if administered properly, did not penetrate the hull but loosened the seams for a considerable distance either side of where it struck.

The penteconter, single-level or double-level, did not command the seas for long. By about 500 BC it had been rendered obsolete by the next great advance in the ancient warship, the creation of the famous trireme.

48 Dionysus and his satyrs travelling in an undecked two-level war galley, probably a triaconter. The upper level rows through ports just under the gunwale, the lower through ports in the side of the hull. Painting on a jug from Tarquinia, Italy. Late 6th century BC.

49 Undecked one-level Greek war galley, probably a penteconter. The oarsmen row from the gunwale. Painting on an Athenian bowl in the Louvre, Paris. Second half of the 6th century BC.

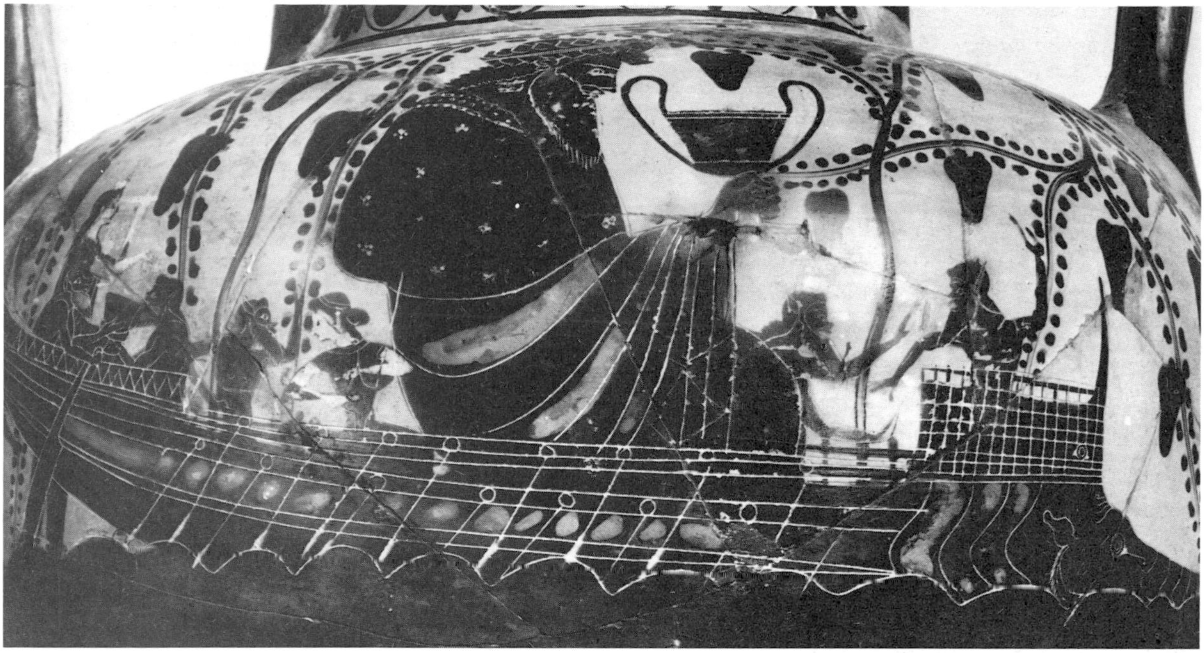

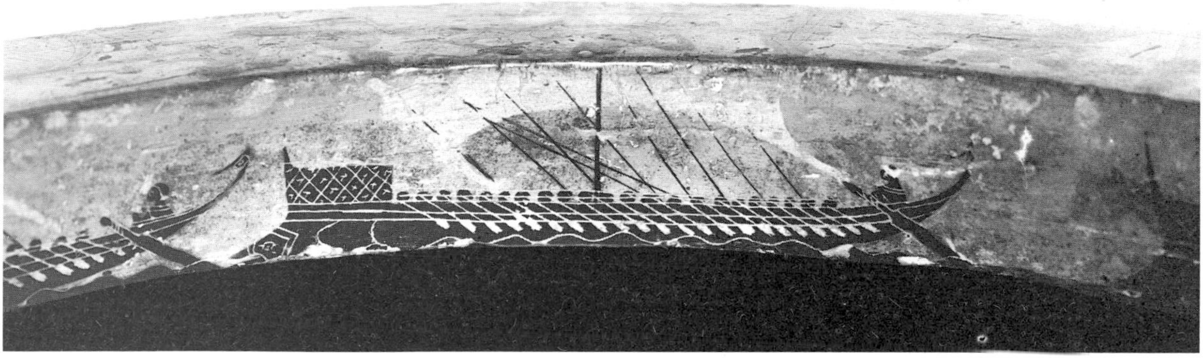

50 Decked one-level Greek war galley, probably a triaconter. A line of marines, protecting themselves with round shields, stands on the deck. Gem in the Metropolitan Museum of Art, New York. Late 6th century BC.

6

The Age of the Trireme

When Greece grew more powerful . . ., with its revenues increasing it went in for the building up of navies and took more to the sea. The Corinthians were the first to turn to ship-design that was very close to the modern fashion, and the earliest Greek triremes were built in Corinth.[1]

So states Thucydides, the great Athenian historian, who wrote in the second half of the fifth century BC, 250 or so years after the events he here describes. In this almost offhand way, he adverts to what was as revolutionary then as the introduction of steam-driven ironclads in the last century. The trireme was destined to rule the Mediterranean waters for almost two centuries, from roughly 500 to shortly before 300 BC, and it continued to serve thereafter as an important unit in all fleets right through the great days of the Roman Empire.

It was during the period from 700 to 500 BC that the Greek city-states gained the power and wealth to which Thucydides refers. Their increased interest in the sea resulted in the planting of dozens of colonies all about the Mediterranean and the Black Sea and the maintaining of active trade with them. Thriving seaports came into being, such as Miletus on the coast of Asia Minor, Corinth and Athens in Greece, Syracuse in Sicily, Marseilles on the south coast of France. Their wealth, as Thucydides remarks, enabled them to build up navies, and the wealthiest of them all, Corinth, was able to launch the costliest warship of all, the trireme. A fleet of penteconters was expensive enough, with its fifty oarsmen per vessel to be paid; a fleet of triremes, as we shall see in a moment, raised the number to 170 rowers per vessel, to say nothing of the higher outlay for construction.

Corinth probably built its first triremes about the middle of the seventh century BC. It took some 200 years before the new war galley finally dominated the fleets. No doubt its formidable price contributed to the delay: naval commanders must have been loath to scrap their familar and quite efficient two-level penteconters for a ship that cost so much more until it had proved itself. By 500 BC it had done so with a vengeance. When, in 480 BC, at the celebrated Battle of Salamis, a Greek fleet some three or four hundred strong squared off against a Persian aggregation at least double that size, on both sides the ship of the line was the trireme.

Since the trireme played so large a role in naval history, it is frequently mentioned by Greek and Roman writers and, as a consequence, we know a good deal more about it than its predecessors. The writers drop remarks about a number of its features, about the behaviour of its rowers, about the contingents of marines, about its performance, about modifications made to it because of combat conditions, and the like. We are particularly well informed about the triremes of the Athenian navy, for they played a leading role in the Peloponnesian War, the struggle that for twenty-seven years, from 431 to 404 BC, Athens and its allies carried on against Sparta, Corinth and other city-states in the Peloponnese and whose story is told in detail by Thucydides and Xenophon, both Athenians. Furthermore, in 1836 workmen digging a foundation at Piraeus, where ancient Athens maintained its naval base, made a unique find: they unearthed some chunks of marble that turned out to have inscribed on them the navy's inventory records for certain years of the fourth century BC; these furnish priceless details about the equipment of triremes.

But no remark in ancient writings, no entry in the naval records, makes clear just what kind of galley the trireme was. 'Trireme' is an English formation from the Latin *triremis* ('three-oared'), a term for the vessel used by Livy, Caesar and other Latin authors. Navy men, Roman as well as Greek, referred to it by its technical name, *trieres*, a word that means 'three-fitted'. Precisely how the trireme was 'three-fitted' has caused a long-standing and heated debate.

The penteconter and triaconter were so called because of the number of rowers in the crew, fifty in the one case, thirty in the other. Obviously the *trieres* was named on some different basis. Ancient writers nowhere bother to make this basis clear, since they were addressing contemporary readers who, completely familiar with the vessel, needed no enlightenment on the point. As we shall see later, in the course of time still larger units named on the same basis came into existence – the *tetreres* ('four-fitted'), *penteres* ('five-fitted'), *hexeres* ('six-fitted'), right up to what must have been a veritable behemoth, a *tessarakonteres* ('forty-fitted').

The earliest theory about these galleys, one that goes back to the fifth century AD, by which time they had become obsolete, was that the numeral referred to the levels of rowers. Thus a *trieres*, it held, had the
rowers arranged in three superimposed levels, a *tetreres* in four, a *penteres* 51
in five, and so on. So far as the trireme was concerned, the theory had

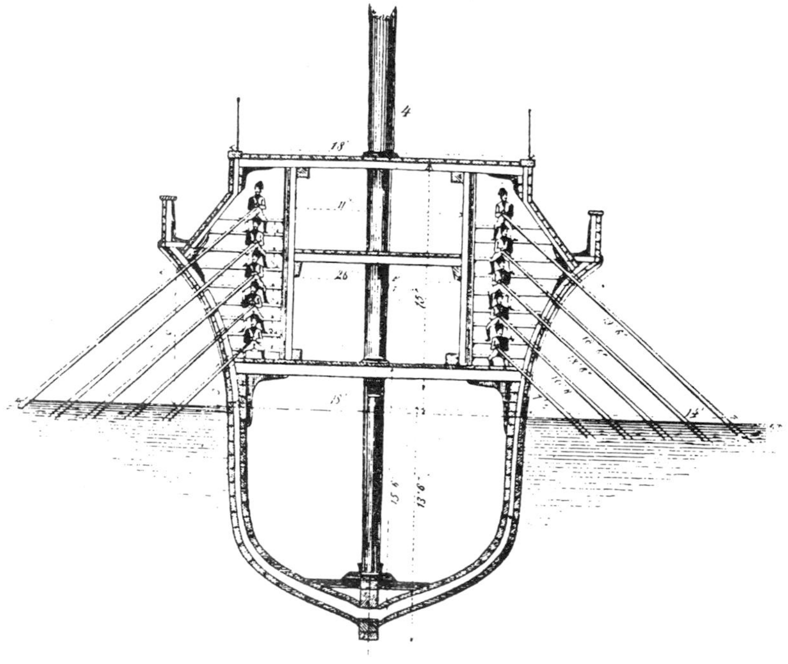

51 A *penteres* as reconstructed by B. Graser in his *De veterum re navali*, published in 1864.

the advantage of agreeing with whatever scanty information was available and of making historical sense: it was logical that, after the two-level galley, the next step would be one with three levels. Of the larger types, practically nothing was known – a state of affairs that the passage of 1500 years has improved but little.

In the early sixteenth century, a rival theory arose. The naval historians of the day were dubious about the feasibility of even a three-level galley, to say nothing of types with still more levels. Furthermore, they were well acquainted with the Venetian galleys described above (Chapter 5), in 45
which the oarsmen were all on one level and gathered into clusters of, usually, three on the same bench. Such a craft could well be described as 'three-fitted'. Why could it not be a descendant of the ancient trireme and reflect, at least in a general way, the same arrangement of rowers?

The theory flourished, although it had absolutely no right to. For one thing, the Venetian style of galley was demonstrably *not* the product of a tradition that reached back to ancient times; indeed, it did not even go back to the Middle Ages. For another, it did not at all fit the information available about the nature of a trireme. Lastly, as time went on, there began to turn up various representations on reliefs and coins and vases 52–3
that almost unmistakably showed galleys with three levels. 56

In 1941, John Morrison, a British classicist with a knowledge of the mechanics of rowing, published an article that went a long way towards putting an end to the seemingly interminable debate. Assembling every scrap of information about the trireme – the remarks in ancient writings, the details from the naval records, all the representations that were relevant – he was able to offer a design for a galley with rowers in three levels that not only squared with all this information but, so far as could be determined from an articulated scale model of one section that he had made up, was eminently workable. Forty years later the issue was put beyond all doubt when Morrison, teaming up with a naval architect, John Coates, worked up plans for a full-scale replica of an Athenian trireme; Morrison supplied his original design, now improved by further dis-

52 Phoenician trireme pictured on a coin from Sidon, dating from 380–374 BC. The artist has clearly indicated the three levels of oars.

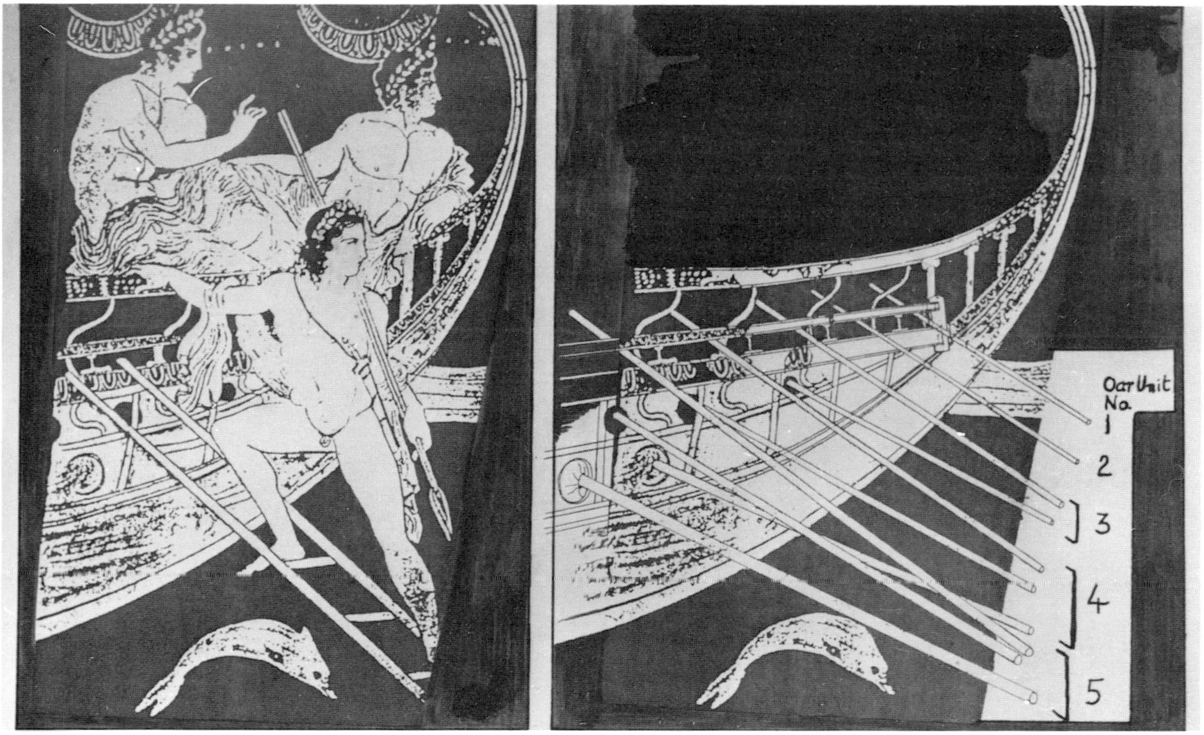

53 The panel to the left is a scene from the story of the Argonauts depicted on a Greek vase of about 400 BC in the Palazzo Iatta at Ruvo, Italy. The artist represents their vessel as a contemporary trireme. We see its port quarter as it lies drawn up on a beach. The ports for the oars are clearly visible; the fuzzy lines running out from the lowest port represent an untied leather sleeve (see Fig. 56). The panel to the right shows a reconstruction by J. F. Coates of how the oars would have fitted. At the stern, where the hull is shallowest, there was room only for rowers in the uppermost level – two of them, one behind the other. In front of these two there was room for a rower in the middle level as well as in the uppermost. From this point on, the hull was deep enough to accommodate men in all three levels, and two such triads are shown in the reconstruction.

coveries, and Coates supplied the modifications dictated by the laws of physics, the properties of materials, and so on. In the summer of 1987 the ship, christened *Olympias*, was launched and put through a series of trials. It performed nobly. VIII, IX

The general dimensions of the triremes of the Athenian navy had been known since 1885 when remains, dating to the fourth century BC, of some of the sheds that had housed them were discovered at Piraeus. Each consisted of a sloping slipway cut in bedrock and separated from its neighbours by a row of columns that supported the roof. The length of the slipways down to the point where they met the water was a little over 121 feet (37 m) and the width between the columns was 19 ft 6 in. (just under 6 m). The *Olympias,* conformably, was given an overall 54
length of 120 ft 9 in. (36.8 m) and a beam of 17 ft 9 in. (5.45 m). On the waterline it measured 105 ft 8 in. by 12 ft (32.2 × 3.62 m), that is, a length to beam ratio of 9 to 1.

And, thanks to the naval records, the number of rowers in each level was known: 31 to a side in the uppermost, 27 in the other two, making 170 in all. Then there were 5 officers, 14 or so marines, various ratings, and seamen for handling sail when it was raised. These, some 30 in all, brought the total crew to 200. Of the rowers, those in the lowermost level were named thalamites since they were seated down in the *thalamos*, 'hold' (their location inspired Aristophanes in his comedy *The Frogs* to pass a crack about the oarsmen's habit of 'breaking wind in the face of

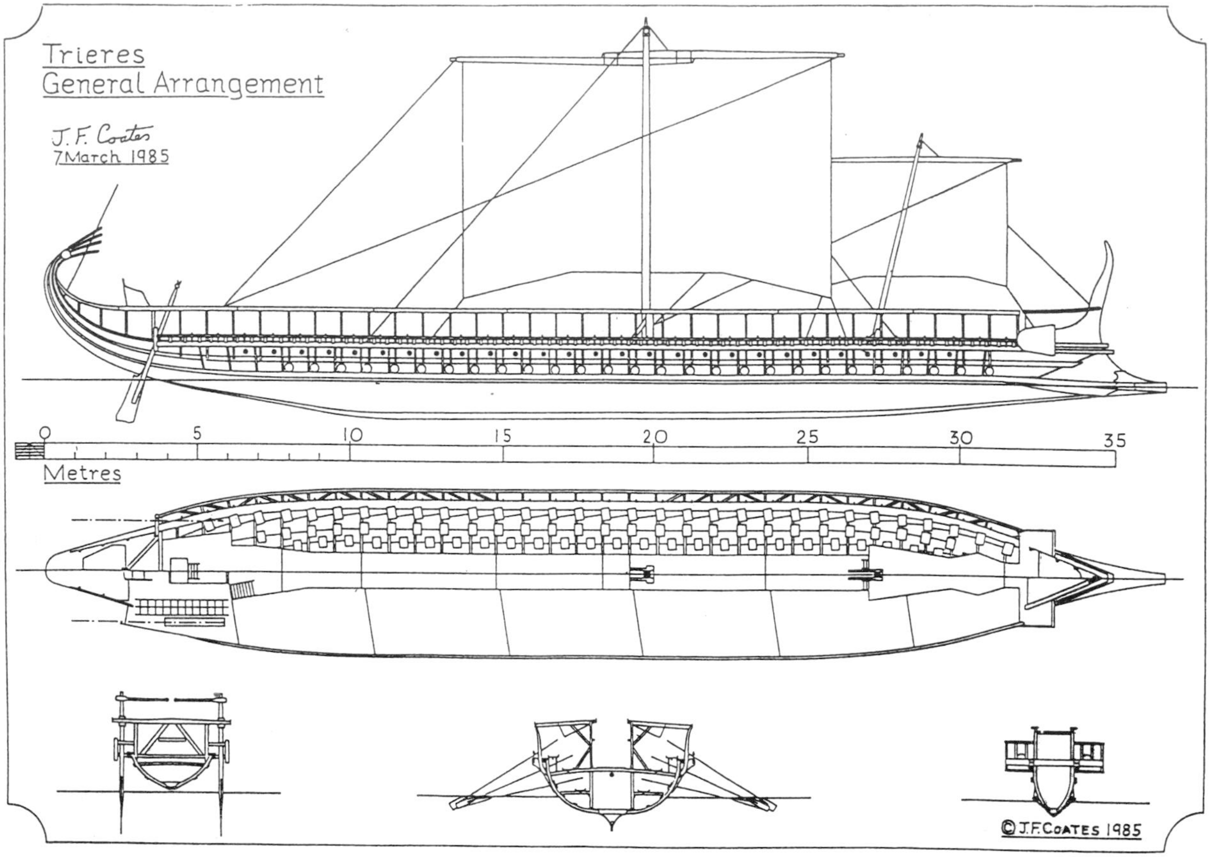
Trieres
General Arrangement
J. F. Coates
7 March 1985
0
5
10
15
20
25
30
35
Metres
© J.F. Coates 1985

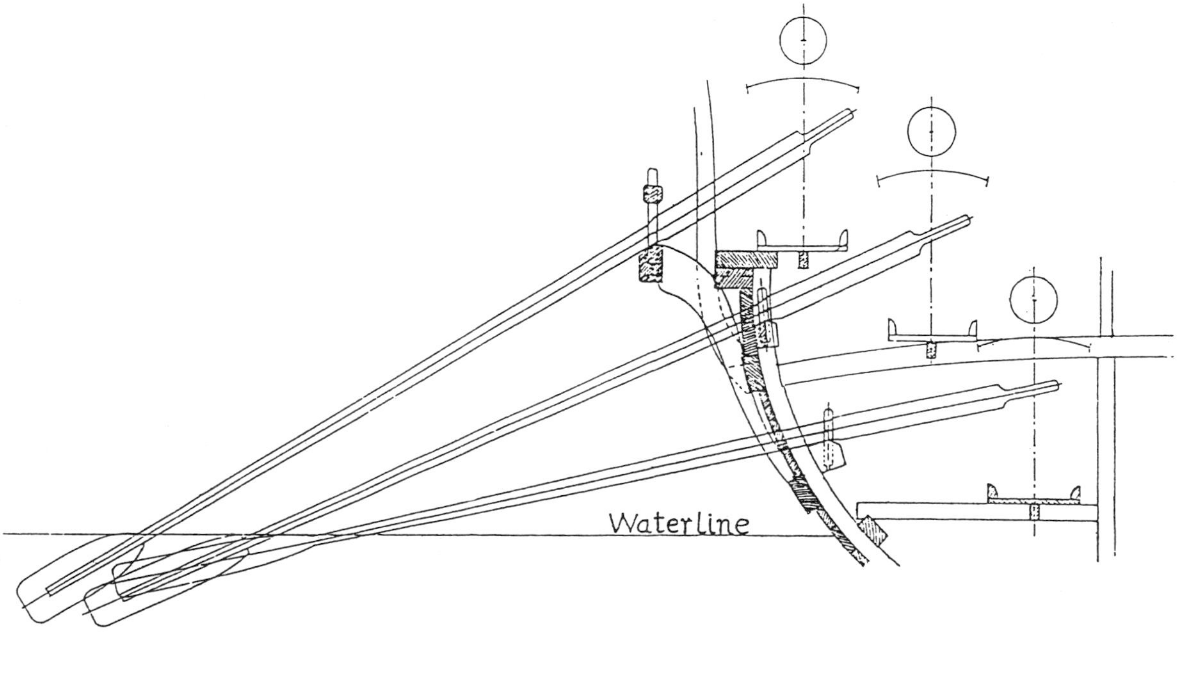
Waterline

54 Plans of the trireme replica *Olympias* (see Colour Plate VIII, opposite p. 128).

55 Plan showing how the oars of the trireme replica strike the water.

the thalamite',[2] a simple-minded joke that has produced much learned
and grave discussion on the part of one-level theorists to prove that the
offenders need not have been rowers sitting in a bank above). Like the
lower bank in the two-level penteconter, the thalamites worked their oars
through ports cut in the side. They were seated so deep in the ship that
the ports were a scant eighteen inches (45 cm) or so above the waterline 55
and the space between the oar and the rim of the port had to be sealed 53, 56
by a leather bag to keep water from coming in. One way the navy had of
disciplining a delinquent was to tie him up with his head sticking out of
the port; in harbour this was probably not much worse than the pillory,
but under way it could be punishing. Above the line of thalamites was
the line of zygites, so called because, like the upper bank in the two-level
penteconter, they sat on the *zyga*, the vessel's thwarts. What distinguished
the trireme from the two-level penteconter was a third line of oarsmen,
the thranites, who worked their oars on an outrigger which ran, following
the curve of the side of the ship, from bow to stern. It was the innovation
of the outrigger that made the trireme possible, as it permitted the
designing of a hull capable of accommodating three lines of oarsmen
without rising inefficiently high above the water. For the three were not
completely superimposed: the thranites, since their oars were pivoted on
the outrigger, were able to be seated outboard of the zygites and only IX
slightly higher, more alongside them than above them. Thus the hull
from the waterline up to the level of the thranite tholes measured but
four feet (1.2 m), and its draft was a little over three and a half. Crews
had no trouble hauling triremes up the slipways into the sheds or, when
cruising, up on a beach.

The oars in all three levels were the same length, about fourteen feet 55
(4.3 m), just about what is standard in naval cutters today, save for a few
at bow and stern where the sides, curving inboard, left less room. These
were slightly shorter, a little over thirteen feet.

The key rowing unit was the group of three consisting of a thranite 53
plus the zygite almost alongside him and the thalamite below him; it was
this triad that gave the vessel its name, 'three-fitted'. There were twenty- 54
seven such triads, with two thranites rowing alone at each end. The oars
were so arranged that the blades entered the water more or less aligned
one behind the other. To accomplish this the oars in the three levels 55
slanted down each at a different angle. The thranite oars, being the
highest, had the steepest angle and hence were the hardest to pull.
Moreover, the thranite was the key member of each triad, for he was the
only one who could see the oars entering the water; the zygite and IX
thalamite rowed blind. As the crews of the *Olympias* soon found out, it was
the thranite's job to monitor the other two, to adjust to any irregularities in
their strokes by seeing to it that his blade always entered the water in the
space between theirs. When, in 415 BC, Athens dispatched a mighty
armada to attack Syracuse in Sicily, 'the thranites', reports Thucydides,

56 The so-called Lenormant relief of about 400 BC, showing the starboard side of a trireme. The uppermost level of rowers is clearly visible, their oars portrayed as slanting lines running from their hands to the water. The middle level is represented by the parallel slanting lines running from just under what appears to be the heaviest wale (but is actually the edge of an outrigger) down to the water. The lowest level is represented by the short parallel slanting lines that seem to emerge from little bulges; these bulges are the artist's way of portraying the leather sleeves attached to and extending from the sides of the ports. They were securely wrapped about the loom of the oar to keep water from coming in through the port. Acropolis Museum, Athens.

'received a bonus on top of their regular pay'[3] – understandably, for they not only had the hardest stroke but were vital to an effective performance.

Some three feet (1 m) above the thranite rowers stretched the *katastroma*, a deck that extended from prow to stern and from gunwale to gunwale. Here the marines took their station, as did the deckhands who handled the lines when the vessel was under sail. The deck was also, so to speak, part of the trireme's armour, sheltering the rowers against the firing of missiles down upon them, while screens, probably of leather, that reached from deck down to gunwale, sheltered them against enemy missiles coming from the side. Vessels so decked and screened were cataphracts, to use the Greek terminology, 'completely fenced in', as against aphracts, open galleys that were 'unfenced'. 56, V

Triremes, like practically all ancient ships, were built shell-first with the planks fastened to each other by multitudinous mortise and tenon joints (see Chapter 3). But since they were so long and narrow, they needed help to keep them from hogging, that is, from drooping at the ends. That was supplied by powerful cables called *hypozomata* ('undergirds'). These ran in the interior of the hull over the centreline from bow to stern and were twisted to the appropriate tension by a sort of tourniquet. When the ship was out of service, they were slacked off or removed. The twisting to proper tension was carried out just before a trireme was put in the water; it was so arduous that it required a sizeable team, and so important that navy regulations specified the minimum number of men allowed to perform it. As might be expected, several spares were carried.

A trireme's engine was its 170 rowers, and the performance of the

Olympias has revealed dramatically how powerful an engine it was. During the trials, despite limited training and the use of oars that were much too heavy, the crew was able to get the vessel to sprint at a speed of 8 knots (proper oars would have permitted much more), to drive the ship for hours at 4 knots with half the oarsmen rowing in turns, and to execute a 180-degree turn in an arc no wider than two and a half ship lengths.

The trireme carried two squaresails, a main and a smaller foresail, and VIII
it travelled under these whenever possible. The *Olympias'* trials showed that it travelled very well, achieving as much as 8 knots with a good wind on a favourable course. The rowers were saved for combat, when a warship operated under oars alone, for, once in action, it had to be ready to head in any direction at a moment's notice and could not possibly depend upon the wind. Moreover, the lines and other equipment would encumber the decks and hinder the movements of the marines. The practice arose of stowing all the sailing gear away before going into battle or, if convenient, leaving it ashore.

Thanks to the naval records, we know precisely what that gear was – indeed, we know all the gear carried by a trireme, whether of rope, cloth or wood. Items of rope and cloth, gathered in the inventories under the heading 'hanging gear', included the 'big sail' (the mainsail) and the 'boat sail' (the foresail) and the lines for these: halyard, two braces, two sheets, two lifts (the lines running from the yard-arms to the tip of the mast to control the slant of the yard), eighteen loops of brails. Also under this heading were eight sets of heavy ropes – no doubt the mooring lines and the cables, with spares, for the two iron anchors that were standard equipment – and several kinds of screens, including those that closed in the sides from deck to gunwale. The very first item in the list of the 'hanging gear' was the *hypozomata*; this pride of place shows how important a piece of equipment they were considered. Under the heading 'wooden gear' were 200 oars of regular size (i.e., 30 spares in addition to the 170 for the crew) plus two oversize oars for steering the ship, the 'big mast' and 'big yard', the 'boat mast' and 'boat yard', two landing ladders, two or three boat poles.

There were five officers aboard a trireme. The highest was the *trierarchos* ('*trieres* captain'). In the Athenian navy this was a political appointee from the ranks of the wealthy whom the state called upon to assume for one year the expense of fitting out and maintaining a trireme. More often than not, he had no naval experience and did not even sail with the ship, leaving the actual command to the next in line, the
kybernetes. The word means 'helmsman', and in early times the *kybernetes* 57
no doubt did handle the helm, but in the triremes of the fifth century BC and later he had more important duties and left the actual steering to quartermasters. When the *trierarchos* was not aboard, he was the commanding officer; otherwise he was the second in command. Below

57 In this picture of a Greek war galley the artist gives prominence to the ship's officers. At the stern, grasping the tiller, is the captain–helmsman; amidships is the rowing officer, looking towards the captain for orders; on the foredeck is the bow officer, also looking towards the captain. Painting on an Athenian vase in the Louvre, Paris. First half of the 6th century BC.

him was the *keleustes* ('timebeater'), a name that also goes back to bygone days when this officer actually beat the time; now he was chief rowing officer, responsible for the training and performance of the oarsmen. Under him was the *pentekontarchos*; the name suggests that he was commander of a penteconter back when that was the ship of the line; in a trireme he had important administrative duties, serving as paymaster, purchasing officer and recruiting officer. Lowest in the hierarchy was the *proreus* or *prorates*, the bow officer, who, stationed on the foredeck, was entrusted with keeping a sharp look-out; this was the first grade a rower ambitious for promotion could hope to achieve. These five grades were, so to speak, the commissioned officers. There were also various ratings: deckhands to handle sail; a ship's carpenter to take care of repairs; quartermasters to take the helm; and – of key importance – the *auletes* ('flautist') or *trieraules* ('*trieres*-flautist') who piped the time for the rowers once the *keleustes* had set the stroke. In some navies the galleys carried a ship's doctor, but there is no indication that this was true of Athens'.

At the Battle of Salamis Athens put 200 triremes into the line, a contingent that required no less than 34,000 rowers. In the fourth century BC its navy had almost double that number of units. Obviously large-scale recruiting must have gone on to keep the benches manned. The city's residents had to fill the ranks of the army as well as the navy; since soldiers supplied their own armour and weapons, it worked out that citizens who could afford the outlay for such items fought in the army and citizens who could not made up the hard core of the rowing crews. But their numbers fell far short of the number required, and navies had to go out and hire the rest. Though the work was arduous and could be dangerous, recruiters seem to have had little difficulty finding applicants. There were plenty of muscular young fellows in the fishing villages of Greece and the islands who knew how to handle an oar and for whom hiring out as a rower offered not only a good salary – a drachma a day, the same as any craftsman got – but also one of the very few avenues of escape from a monotonous life of grinding poverty. For there were not many ways an unskilled worker could earn a wage in ancient Greece, since such labour was mostly done by slaves.

Contrary to what is often thought, ancient states did not man their warships with slave rowers, except in very unusual circumstances. For example, when in 406 BC, toward the end of the Peloponnesian War, Athens faced a life-and-death situation and had run out of all other sources of manpower, the city turned to slaves to fill the gaps in the benches and rewarded all who served with freedom. Using state-owned slaves made no economic sense. The purchase of a crew would require a massive investment, since able-bodied slaves were by no means cheap, and the cost of any killed in action would have to be written off as a total loss; on top of that, all would have to be fed and housed every day of the year every year of their lives whether there was a war going on or not.

The hired oarsmen were paid only when they actually rowed, and their death cost their employers nothing. Slaves were occasionally to be found in the rowing crews, but these were just another form of hired oarsmen, privately owned slaves who knew how to row and whose owners profited by renting them to the state and pocketing the wages they earned.

In the great days of sail a few centuries ago it was common practice to keep back part of a seaman's wage and hand it over only at the end of the voyage; this not only ensured that he would not squander his total earnings on liquor and prostitutes *en route* but also would think twice before jumping ship and thereby forfeiting the balance due to him. Ancient navies apparently had the same problem and met it the same way, at least according to what a disaffected Athenian admiral told the paymaster of the Peloponnesian fleet. He induced him, Thucydides reports,

> to cut the wage from a drachma to three obols [i.e., half a drachma] and not to pay it out regularly, ... [explaining] that the Athenians with their long experience in naval matters pay their own men only three obols, not because of lack of funds but to keep the men from being corrupted by having too much; otherwise some would harm their bodies by squandering money on the sort of things that injure the health and others, with no pay owing to them to serve as a sort of hostage, would jump ship.[4]

The rowers, in addition to their salary, received a maintenance allowance, and this brings us to one of the most curious features of ancient naval logistics, the cavalier fashion in which the vital matter of feeding the crews was treated. The ancient Greek's diet was simple, little more than grain for some form of porridge or bread, some legumes, a handful of figs or olives. But the cramped quarters of a trireme had scant space for supplies of even this meagre fare, certainly for anything more than a day or two. The solution was to give the men an allowance and send them off to buy their own food. When a fleet was back at its base, there was no problem: the citizens who lived near the waterfront ate and slept at home, while those who did not, along with the hired foreigners, slept in barracks and bought their food at various nearby stores and markets. The problem arose when the ships were in service. They never ventured far from shore. For one thing, the open sea was not for the likes of light and elongated war galleys packed from keel to deck with human beings. For another, every night fleet commanders had to reckon on landing at some place where the ships could be hauled up so that the men could eat and sleep ashore. What is more, the place had to be near a settlement that had a market, for, once the men had pulled their boats up on the beach, off they would go to the market, buy food, and bring it back to cook and eat beside the ships. Apparently, thousands of hungry men could suddenly descend upon a town on the coast, even one of modest size, and find enough on hand in the market to meet their needs. It boggles the imagination, but that is the way the crews were fed. Consider the account given by Thucydides of what happened once in the town of Eretria in Euboea, which had long been subject to Athens. In 411 BC, when Athens, after two decades of war, was manifestly weakening, the townspeople saw a chance to revolt: they worked out a plan with the commander of a Peloponnesian fleet to get rid of an Athenian contingent of thirty-six ships that was in their harbour. On the appointed day, they secretly kept all vendors away from the marketplace, which must have been near the waterfront, and when the Athenian crews, presumably over 7000 strong, 'happened to be buying provisions for their midday meal, not at the market, for the Eretrians had seen to it that nothing was being offered for sale there, but at the houses at the furthest edge of town',[5] they sent a signal to the Peloponnesian fleet lying in the offing and it was able to descend on the Athenian ships while numbers of the rowers were still scuttling back from their shopping. It inflicted a smashing defeat, capturing no less than twenty-two of the undermanned Athenian galleys. In this instance thousands of men had been doing their buying not even at a regular market but at miscellaneous households!

Or consider what finally brought about the end of the Peloponnesian War; in the light of the savage fighting that had gone on for so long, it was anticlimactic, almost farcical. In September of 405 BC Athens sent the entire navy, 180 triremes, to the Dardanelles to ensure that freighters carrying grain from southern Russia to feed the city would get through safely. Athens' high command had its share of boneheaded admirals, but those at the head of this fleet surpassed them all. They chose to draw up the force on a remote beach on the northern shore with no market in the vicinity; the town of Sestus, almost two miles away, was the nearest place where the crews could buy food. An experienced ex-admiral, who happened to be living nearby, warned them of the danger involved in staying at such a place; they told him to mind his own business. The Peloponnesian fleet had camped at Lampsacus, a well-stocked city on the opposite shore. The next morning both sides manned their ships, and the Athenians rowed up to the enemy formation and offered battle. Lysander, its canny admiral, held off, and when the Athenians went back to their beach, he sent scouts to keep an eye on them, at the same time holding his own men at their battle stations. For four days in a row the procedure was repeated: the fleets rowed out and faced each other, Lysander backed off, the Athenians returned to their beach, and the crews trudged off to Sestus to do their marketing with Lysander's scouts keeping a sharp eye on their movements. On the fifth day, as Xenophon, the Athenian historian whose narrative includes the years in question, tells it, he instructed the scouts,

> that, as soon as they spotted the Athenians out of their ships and getting scattered along the road, something that was happening more and more every day since they were buying their food from far off . . ., they should sail

back toward him and when halfway across should hoist a shield [to flash a signal by catching the sun, like a heliograph].[6]

They did as instructed, Lysander immediately dashed out, and, without losing a man, he captured practically the whole Athenian fleet since, 'with its rowers scattered all over, some ships had only two levels manned, some only one, and in some the benches were totally empty.'[7] It was probably the easiest and most spectacular victory in the history of naval warfare. Only nine Athenian craft escaped. They happened to be under the command of Conon, an alert and able naval officer, who managed to get his men aboard and raise sail on his tiny flotilla quickly enough to make a getaway. Lysander, stripped for action, had left all his sailing gear behind in port, so Conon, in a move reminiscent of the bandits in a Western film who run off with their victims' horses in order to forestall chase, took the time to stop at the enemy's anchorage for a few minutes and cart off all the sails that had been left there.

Feeding the crews may have been handled haphazardly, but maintaining the ships was finely organised. When not in service, triremes were hauled out of the water into roofed sheds, with the 'wooden gear' stored 58
alongside and the 'hanging gear' removed for storage in special warehouses. This was to prevent the galleys from getting waterlogged or having the bottom fouled with marine growth, either of which would reduce the vessels' speed and manoeuvrability and diminish their effectiveness in battle. When cruising, commanders looked for an opportunity to haul their ships up on a beach and dry them out. Condition was so important that the Athenian navy, for example, had an elaborate classification of its ships based on it. At the top were the 'selects'; then came 'firsts', 'seconds', 'thirds', and 'old'. The 'selects' were probably vessels that had been recently built and were in perfect shape. Since triremes lasted some twenty years or more, those classified 'old' were presumably nearing that age, and the 'firsts', 'seconds' and 'thirds' must have represented grades in between.

Although all triremes were basically alike, so that, for example, a commander who had captured some enemy units could incorporate them into his own forces, there was variation from navy to navy. The Athenian navy emphasised ram attacks; since these called for speed and manoeuvrability, it favoured hulls that were built as lightly as possible, held the number of marines to a minimum – just ten spearmen and three or four archers – and trained the rowing crews to a fine edge. The Corinthians, not as adept at ramming as the Athenians, emphasised grappling and boarding and so went in for heavier vessels carrying a greater number of marines.

In addition to ships of the line, navies had at least two types of service triremes. One was the 'soldier-vessel', a troop transport, which was rowed by the thranites alone, thereby leaving the benches of the zygites and thalamites free for passengers. The other was the 'horse-transport'. These

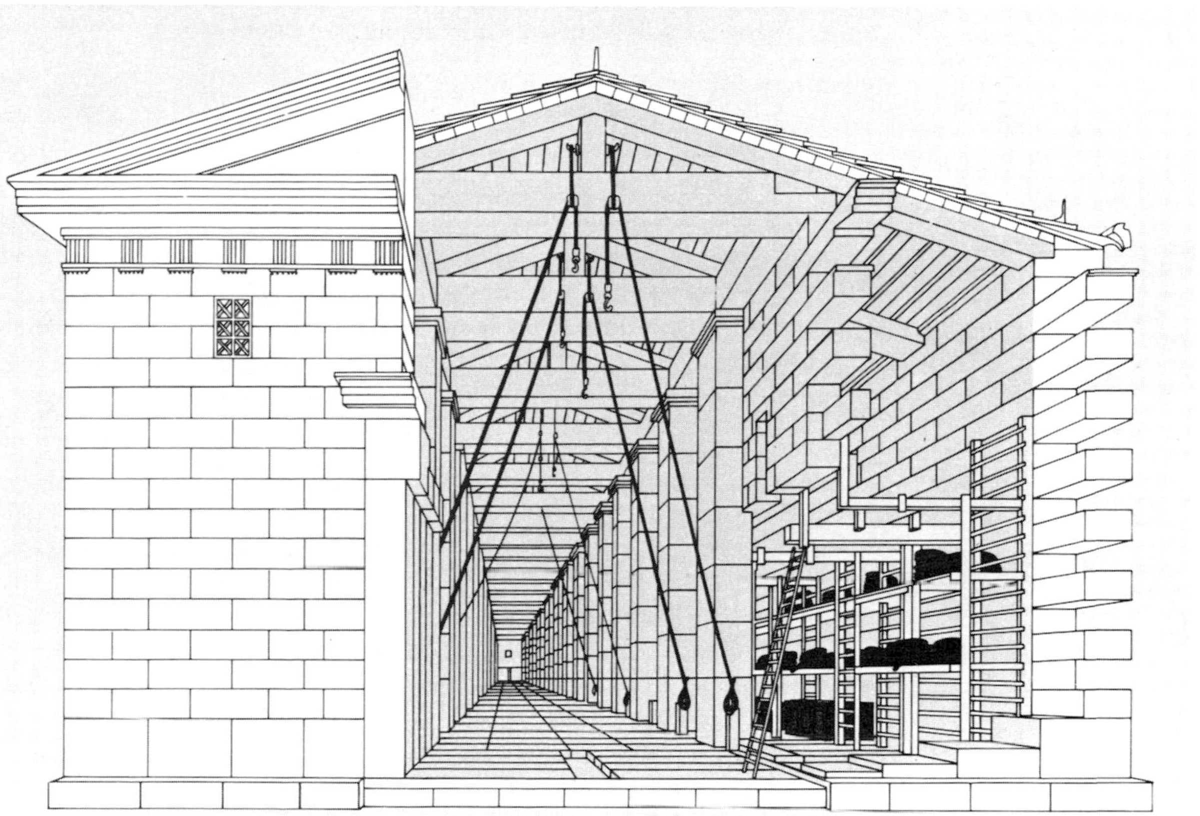

58 Reconstruction of the shed built at Piraeus in the 4th century BC to house the gear of the triremes of the Athenian fleet.

were made out of old triremes by removing the two lower levels of seats and converting the space into stalls for thirty horses; as in the troop transports, the rowing was done by the thranites.

The trireme's reason for being, in a real sense, was the ram at its bow. Yet for a long time all we knew about this vital element in a war galley's make-up was its general shape. Then, in 1980, Israeli marine archaeologists had the good fortune to come upon an actual specimen in the waters off Athlit near Haifa. It was in perfect condition and, wedged inside it, were the bow timbers that it had enclosed. The Athlit ram is a 59, 60
superbly cast, mighty sheath of bronze that weighs close to half a ton. Although it almost certainly came from a ship somewhat larger than a trireme, it provides an idea of how big a trireme's ram must have been. The designers of the *Olympias* gave their vessel a ram weighing around 200 pounds (90 kg); such a size is, of course, merely an educated guess, but obviously a good one since the ship performs so well with that amount of weight at its prow.

The ram on the sixth-century penteconters ended in a squarish blunt 48–50,
face (see Chapter 5). By the time of the Peloponnesian War, perhaps VII
even before, another shape had been developed, the shape exemplified

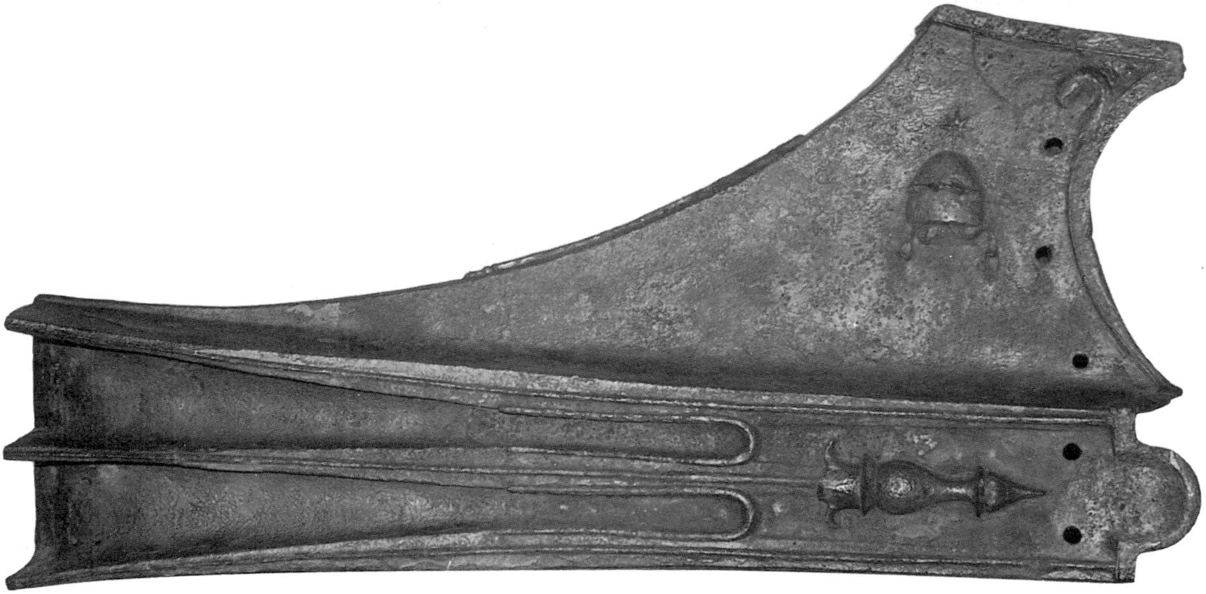

59 The bronze ram found off Athlit, Israel. It is 7 ft 5 in. (2.26 m) long, 30 in. (76 cm) at its widest point, $37\frac{3}{4}$ in. (96 cm) at its highest point, and weighs 1023 lb (465 kg). Probably first half of the 2nd century BC.

by the Athlit ram, which ends in three horizontal fins crossed down the 60
centre by a solid vertical section. This shape inflicted a blow just as damaging as the earlier shape but reduced the danger of penetrating and thereby sticking fast. The ram was a warship's most expensive item of equipment. Not only did it require great amounts of copper but also a high level of metallurgical expertise and complicated foundry facilities, for, to judge from the Athlit example, rams were cast in one piece.

It took a finely trained crew to exploit this weapon. The blow had to be delivered in just the right way or it could end up being as disastrous to the attacker as to the victim. Once the commander of a galley had selected a target, he passed the word to his rowing officer to order maximum speed and kept this speed up until his ship was at the proper point for entering into the final approach. At this precise juncture the vessel had to cut back to what we may call 'ramming speed', and at 'ramming speed' drive in for the kill. Then, at the moment of impact, the crew had to switch to backing water in order to thrust their vessel back until it was in the clear, ready to turn to another target if the blow it had just delivered proved fatal or to charge in to ram again if it had not. The 'ramming speed' had to be calculated to a nicety. It had to be the maximum possible for delivering an effective blow that would still enable the oarsmen to switch efficiently and swiftly at the vital moment from forward motion to back-watering; the quick switch was all-important, because, if the attacker lingered too long, the victim would have time to throw over grappling irons, hold him fast, and turn the encounter into a fight between the marines on both sides. The speed had to be the maximum possible for delivering a blow in which the ram smashed upon the enemy's hull with the desired effect but did not punch into it or too

60 The Athlit ram viewed from the front.

far into it, because, if that happened, the ram might stick fast or, through twisting, break off, and either spelled disaster.

In a sea battle the sides usually faced one another in line abreast – two long lines each with its prows aimed menacingly at the other. Fighting started when commanders saw likely targets for attack and darted forward to ram them. If one side did not specialise in ramming and hence boasted no great skill at it, it would stolidly wait, hoping to ward off a serious blow and to get a chance to close in and grapple; this age-old type of naval combat, galleys coming together to let the men on the decks settle the issue, was by no means rendered obsolete through the introduction of the ram, which simply offered an alternative way of fighting. If both sides were skilled at ramming, the commanders went at each other like fencers: there would be sudden dashes forward, sometimes intended and sometimes feints, sudden retreats, more forward dashes, and so on. They avoided ramming prow to prow: there was little to gain that way, since the forward part of an ancient galley was its strongest, built of massive timbers and powerfully braced.

A galley's most vulnerable areas were the sides or stern. One way of getting at these weak points was to carry out the manoeuvre the Greeks called a *periplus*, a 'sailing around'. One side, usually the side with more ships and hence a longer line, would send galleys racing around the end of the enemy line; if they succeeded, they would turn and hit his vessels from the rear. Another way, even more deadly but harder to execute, was the *diekplus*, the 'breaking through'. In this manoeuvre a ship dashed right through the enemy line, wheeled about after getting through, and, as in the *periplus*, took the enemy ships in the stern. A variant was to start the dash through but, just after passing an enemy prow, swiftly angle over and hit the ship obliquely, in such a way as to run the ram along the side and shear off the oars.

The Athenian navy entered the Peloponnesian War with by far the finest navy afloat, one that had developed to the highest degree the art of fighting with the ram. Thucydides' pages record some striking victories it achieved in the early years of the struggle, when the commanders of the Corinthian and other navies opposing it had not yet devised effective defences against this skilled antagonist. In 429 BC, for example, an Athenian contingent of twenty triremes beat a Peloponnesian fleet more than twice that size. The Peloponnesians, in order to avoid at all costs falling victim to an Athenian *diekplus*, put their fleet in a circle, with five ships as a reserve in the centre and the others rayed out like the spokes of a wheel; their rams, in other words, bristled in all directions. The commander of the squadron arrayed against them was Phormio, Athens' Horatio Nelson. He drew up his vessels in column, formed a ring around the wheel, and kept circling around it. He could not have put his ships in a more perilous position, for he was deliberately exposing their sides to the enemy's rams, but he reckoned that, with his well-trained crews, he could give the order to spin about and get out of ramming range in time. He also counted on the springing up of the morning breeze and the problems that this would create for the dense enemy formation. It came up right on schedule, and, as he had reckoned, caused the ships in the wheel to foul each other; soon they were jammed together so closely that they had no room for working the oars. At that point the Athenians turned from column to line abreast, drilled in, and seized a dozen prizes before the enemy could shake loose.

An even more spectacular feat came not long after. The Peloponnesians waited until they outnumbered the little Athenian squadron not two to one but four to one. They attacked and, with these odds, soon had victory in their grasp: they captured nine triremes and went in savage pursuit of the rest. As the Athenians sweated at the oars to escape, one of their ships lagged behind. An enemy vessel pressed forward to leap upon it. It so happened that a big freighter was lying at anchor in the open roadstead right in the way. The Athenian skipper headed straight for it, but, instead of continuing on past it, made a lightning turn around it which put him in perfect ramming position: he struck his pursuer square amidships. This was too much for the crews of the other enemy galleys. They sat at their oars dumbfounded and, before they could get moving again, the Athenian squadron stopped its flight, wheeled, charged, and sank six of their craft.

Athens' enemies eventually worked out some defences. One was to reinforce the bows of their triremes so massively that a blow there was bound to damage the attacker. Another was to avoid at all costs combat in open waters where the skilled Athenian crews had plenty of room to carry out their intricate manoeuvres. Best of all was to entice the Athenians into a fight in closed waters where they were denied the freedom of action that their tactics required. On one crucial occasion the Athenians allowed this to happen, and the result was a complete and costly defeat. In 415 BC Athens sent out a mighty expedition, a powerful army accompanied by an equally powerful fleet, to capture Syracuse, the foremost city in Sicily. The expedition made camp on the shore of the Great Harbour alongside the city. Things did not go too well; reinforcements had to be sent out, and, by 413 BC, the expedition found itself fighting for its own survival. At one point the Athenians let the enemy carry out an action which signed their fleet's death warrant: they let the Syracusans plug the mouth of the harbour with a line of boats linked together. Now the Athenians, with their light units designed for manoeuvre and ramming, for action where there was plenty of room, had to fight against the ships of the Syracusans, which had bows bulging with bulky timbers, on the Syracusans' terms, bottled up in the waters of the harbour. As Thucydides tells it:

> A maximum number of ships fought in a minimum space, for the two sides together numbered just short of two hundred. Ram attacks were few, since there was no chance for backing water or carrying out a *diekplus*. Collisions were frequent as ship smashed into ship in attempts to flee or to carry on pursuit. As a ship bore down, the men on the deck hurled javelins and fired arrows and stones at it. When two ships came together, the fighting men, in hand to hand combat, struggled to board the others' ship. Often, because of the tight space, a ship that struck another was itself struck, and at times two or even more vessels were locked in combat about one ship.[8]

Despite its devastating defeat in the Peloponnesian War, Athens was able to make an amazing naval comeback. In the fourth century BC it built itself an even greater navy, made up as before almost wholly of triremes. But elsewhere the emphasis was moving in a different direction, towards heavier units that carried larger contingents of marines. By the end of the century the trireme had abdicated its rule of the seas, giving way to warships that dwarfed it in size and power.

7

The Age of the Supergalleys

The trireme came into being in a world dominated by city-states, nations that consisted of no more than a city and the territory immediately surrounding it. Such small polities necessarily had but limited resources; only a few could afford a navy of any size. One great and rich empire did exist at the time – Persia – but its location determined its destiny as primarily a land power; when it needed a fleet it commandeered squadrons from the Greek and Phoenician coastal city-states under its domination.

What enabled the city-state of Athens in the fifth century BC to build up its formidable navy was its position as the head of a defence league that embraced most of the important Greek city-states in the Aegean area, both on the islands and along the coasts. The prime purpose of the league was to share the expense of maintaining a powerful fleet, each member contributing in proportion to its size a certain number of ships or amount of money; when Athens, the biggest and most important member, took what was intended as a voluntary association and converted it into a compulsory union under Athenian domination, the league fleet became in effect Athens' fleet. Sparta and the other city-states that opposed Athens in the Peloponnesian War were finally able to destroy this navy only by talking Persia into giving them the funds for the construction of one that could match it.

Early in the fourth century BC, Athens began the rebuilding of the league and was so successful that by 330 BC it again possessed the biggest fleet on the waters, boasting some 400 triremes. Less than a decade later not only had that mighty aggregation been wiped out, but the trireme had lost forever its commanding place in the hierarchy of ancient warships. For a different world had come into being, in which the nature and size of the dominant powers had changed radically and, inevitably, so had the nature and size of navies.

The first indications of what this world would be like appeared in the west, when Syracuse, the principal Greek city-state in Sicily, ceased to be a democracy and fell under the autocratic rule of Dionysius I. By gradually extending his sway over almost all the other Greek communities on the island, Dionysius made himself lord of a veritable empire which yielded him revenues far richer than any individual city-state could supply. This enabled him to finance a navy that at his death in 367 BC numbered about 300 units and included not only triremes but two types of even bigger warship, the *tetreres* ('four-fitted') and the *penteres* ('five-fitted'); indeed, he is credited with the invention of the latter. Then, in 334 BC, Alexander the Great led an army out of his homeland of 61
Macedon, north of Greece, into Asia Minor and launched the spectacular campaign that brought him to the borders of India. It set in motion political, economic and cultural forces that transformed the world into which he had been born.

61 LEFT Alexander the Great (356–323 BC). Portrait on a coin in the British Museum.

62 RIGHT Demetrius I of Macedonia (336–283 BC). Portrait on a coin in the British Museum.

63 LEFT Ptolemy I (366(?)–282 BC). Portrait on a coin in the British Museum.

That world had been a world of city-states. When he died in 323 BC, Alexander was ruler of an empire reaching from Greece to India; what Dionysius had once held was but a principality in comparison. Vast Persia was merely a part of it, and the Greek and Phoenician city-states that had figured so prominently in history up to then had either been swallowed up in it or were dominated by it. But only an Alexander was capable of holding this huge realm together. At his death it broke apart – not, however, back into the small political fragments that had preceded his rise but into great kingdoms ruled by his former generals. The next segment of ancient history, the Hellenistic Age as it is called, which embraces the three centuries after Alexander's death, is largely the story of how these men, fiercely ambitious and with a lifetime of experience in leading massive armies, divided up his empire and implacably fought one another – first they and then their successors – to keep or expand what they held. The rivalry went on until Rome put an end to it by conquering their territories one by one.

Two decades of warfare among the half-dozen or more original contenders thinned the ranks to three major figures, who succeeded in founding dynasties that lasted. Grizzled, one-eyed Antigonus and his
brilliant son Demetrius for a short time held the lion's share of Alexander's 62
empire, but their progeny, the Antigonids, eventually ended up with
just Macedon and parts of Greece. Bull-necked, jutting-jawed Ptolemy 63
cannily saw to it that Egypt, richest of all the lands Alexander had conquered, fell to his share and solidly established his family on the throne. His was the longest-lived of the great Hellenistic dynasties; it stayed in power right down to 30 BC when Cleopatra, besieged by Roman armies, pressed an asp to her bosom and the rule passed into Roman hands. The third, Seleucus, founded the Seleucid dynasty, whose base was Syria and Mesopotamia.

Seleucus, with a widespread and turbulent territory to administer, was fully occupied on land and for the most part left the sea to the others. Antigonus was quick to perceive the advantage of controlling the waters of the Aegean and eastern Mediterranean, and with the aid of Demetrius, a bold and imaginative designer of mighty siege machines as well as mighty war galleys, set about building a naval force that would outclass every other afloat. Ptolemy and his successor, Ptolemy II, felt compelled to keep abreast, and this touched off an arms race that led to what was to be the high-water mark in the history of oared warships. The rivals poured out immense sums of money. Over and above the cost of the huge vessels they kept launching, they had to pay the huge crews needed to row them. Only autocratic rulers of great kingdoms were in a position to bear such expense.

Since his homeland of Macedon was exclusively a land power, Alexander embarked on his career of conquest without a navy. As he swept over the Greek cities on the coast of Asia Minor and then the Phoenician cities of the Levant, he commandeered the squadrons these maintained and thereby put together a fleet that reached the respectable total of 240 units and, in a battle off the island of Amorgos in 322 BC, was able to end once and for all Athens' days as a naval power. By this time the units larger than the trireme that Dionysius had introduced into Syracuse's fleet, *tetrereis* and *pentereis* – 'fours' and 'fives', as we may call them for convenience – were to be found in increasing numbers in all up-to-date navies. Athens, for example, as the naval records reveal, in 330 BC had eighteen 'fours' alongside the 400 triremes that made up the bulk of its forces; by 325 the number of 'fours' had grown to fifty, and seven 'fives' had been added. Sometime before his death in 344 BC, Dionysius' son and successor, Dionysius II, introduced 'sixes' into the Syracusan navy.

Then the rivalry between the Ptolemies and Antigonus and Demetrius got under way and the speed of change became furious. Ptolemy had managed to get his hands on Alexander's fleet when the great commander died; its biggest units were 'fives'. In 315 Antigonus and Demetrius constructed a fleet which, to outclass it, included 'sevens'. Demetrius then kept launching ever larger ships until, by 301 at least, he had 'eights', 'nines', 'tens', 'elevens', even a 'thirteen'. In 288 he upped the ante still further with a 'fifteen' and a 'sixteen', sizes that, as Plutarch reports in his *Life of Demetrius*, 'no mortal had ever before seen'; what is more, 'the beauty of the ships was by no means neglected, nor did they lose in usefulness because of the vast scale of their construction. As a matter of fact, their speed and performance were more remarkable than their size.'[1]

The first Ptolemy kept up as best he could, and his successor, Ptolemy II (282–246 BC), even forged ahead with first a 'twenty' and then two 'thirties'. The summit was reached with the launching by Ptolemy IV (222–205 BC) of a 'forty'. This behemoth never saw action and probably from the outset was intended only for display: the fourth Ptolemy had a weakness for monumentally expensive showpieces.

A proper navy included not merely one or two of the oversize galleys but squadrons of them. The fleet of Ptolemy II, for example, at its strongest had two 'thirties', one 'twenty', four 'thirteens', two 'twelves', fourteen 'elevens', thirty 'nines', thirty-seven 'sevens', five 'sixes', and 224 'fours', triremes, and smaller types.

What was the nature of these mighty ships? What principle lay behind the numbers in their nomenclature? The few surviving representations that may portray them provide no clue, nor do the mentions of them in ancient writings. We must proceed largely by guesswork, starting with what we know about the trireme and trying to make sense of the numbers. In doing so we must bear in mind that, save for the 'forty', these vessels were not experiments or showpieces; they saw action in all the battles of the age. Plutarch's remark cited above attests to the efficiency of even such large units as the 'fifteen' and 'sixteen'.

In the last century a school of thought arose whose members worked

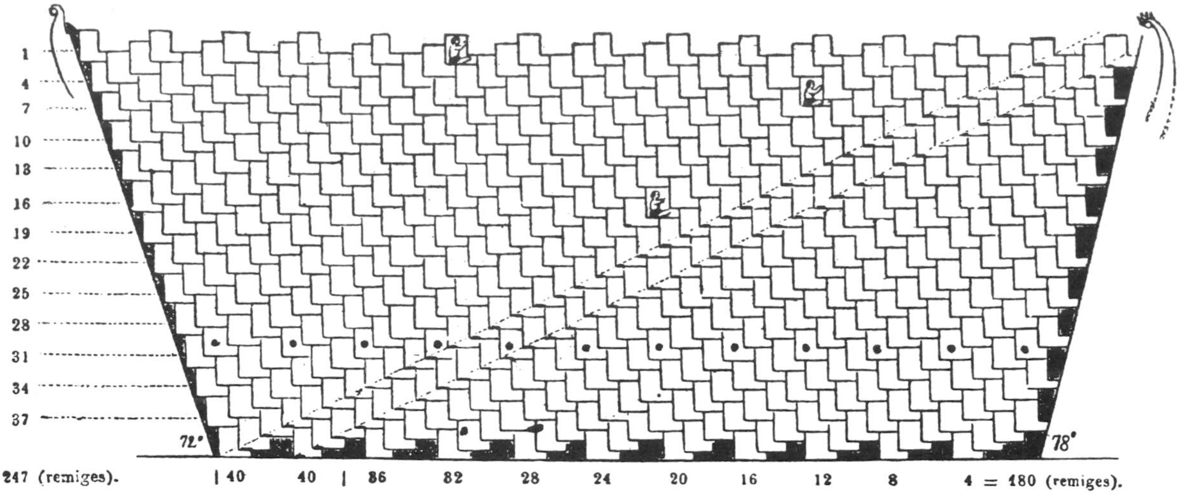

64 The 'forty' of Ptolemy IV as reconstructed by B. Graser in his *De veterum re navali*, published in 1864. The numbers along the left and bottom refer to the total of rowers in the line which starts where the number is placed and slants upward to the right. The longest such line, from the vessel's forefoot at the lower left-hand corner to the stern ornament in the upper right-hand corner, has forty rowers.

on the assumption that a trireme was so called because it had three levels of rowers one above the other, and they resolutely extended this assumption to all the larger sizes. To them a 'four' was so called because it had four superimposed levels, a 'five' because it had five, and so on 51 right up to the 'forty' of Ptolemy IV. They were undisturbed by the patent fact that the monsters coming off their drawing boards could 64 hardly stand up to a stiff breeze, much less carry out the manoeuvring ascribed to them in accounts of ancient naval actions. In the early part of this century a school of thought arose that went in exactly the opposite direction. Its members worked on the assumption that ancient galleys were never more than single-level, including the trireme, and therefore all the sizes recorded, from the smallest to the biggest, had to be single-level. In their view a 'four' was powered by a line of long oars each manned by four men, a 'five' by a line manned by five men, a 'six' by a line manned by six men, and so on. The theory had one strong argument in its favour: this was the way galleys were rowed in the later great age of 44 the oared warship, the sixteenth to the eighteenth century. However, the argument could be extended only to sizes up to the 'eight', for the seamen of that age found out that they could not go beyond eight men to an oar; that was the limit. What, then, was the nature of the 'tens', 'elevens', and bigger galleys launched by Demetrius and the Ptolemies? What was the 'forty' of Ptolemy IV? The only solution this school had to offer was that in such vessels the oars were arranged in clusters, that a 'sixteen', for example, had eight-man oars arranged in clusters of two. This was clearly a solution born of desperation, since there was no reason to group oars in that way – nothing at all was to be gained by it.

Both schools of thought started from wrong assumptions. The first erred in assuming that the ancients built galleys with more than three levels of oarsmen. They never went above three; even the monster 'forty' went up only to a line of thranites, just like a trireme. The second erred

in assuming that the ancients never built galleys with more than one level of oarsmen. As has been shown in the previous chapters, they built, no question about it, two-level and three-level galleys. Both schools, 48, 56
moreover, were unaware that, as we have seen (Chapter 6), a trireme – a 'three', so to speak – got its name from the triad made up of a thranite 53
oarsman and the zygite and thalamite just below him. It follows that a 'four' should get its name from a similar group made up of four members, a 'five' from a group made up of five members, and so on.

When Dionysius introduced 'fours' and 'fives' into the Syracusan fleet the innovation, so far as we can tell, did not materially affect naval warfare. Nor did things change noticeably even after these units entered most other fleets, those of Athens or the Phoenician cities. In the light of this, the simplest and most reasonable explanation would be that they were modifications of the trireme. A 'four' could have been a trireme slightly adapted so that two men could be put on each thranite oar. 65
Similarly a 'five' could have been a trireme adapted to take two men on each zygite oar as well as thranite. When Dionysius II introduced the 'six' he might merely have carried this procedure to its logical conclusion by putting two men on each oar in all three levels. This, however, was as far as the ancient naval designers could have gone in increasing oar power by more or less minor adjustments to the trireme. Going further brought in its wake fundamental changes.

In the ancient galleys that preceded the trireme, and in the trireme itself, there was but one rower to each oar and he rowed from a seated

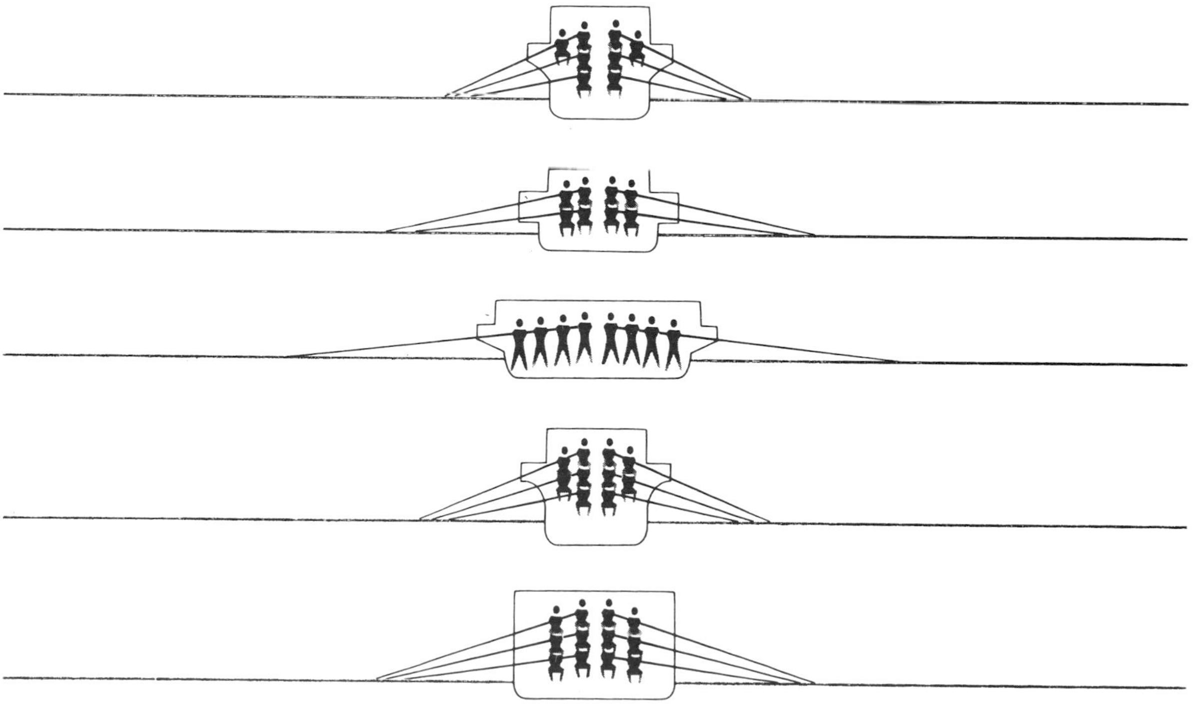

65 Possible arrangements of the rowers of a 'four', 'five' and 'six'. The upper three show a three-level, two-level and one-level 'four'. The lower two show a three-level 'five' and a three-level 'six'.

position, like the crews of today's racing shells. Adding a second man to an oar does not change this; a pair can still row seated. But adding a third man does, and radically. To accommodate three men, an oar becomes so long that the men can no longer row seated: to dip the blade in the water they must rise to their feet and raise their arms, and to deliver the stroke they must throw themselves back on the bench. This is the way the great multiple-rower sweeps of the galleys of the Knights of Malta, of the Papacy and the other navies of the time were operated. The Italian term for such a sweep was *remo scaloccio*, 'big-ladder oar'; it perhaps got the name because, to operate it, the rowers climbed, ladder-like, from the 44
deck on to what was called the *pedagna*, then higher to the *banchetta*, and then fell back on their bench. Since no ancient galley ever went above three levels of oarsmen, in a 'seven' one of the levels must have had at least three men to an oar – three men, say, on each thranite oar and two men on each zygite and thalamite – and the added man must have brought in its wake a switch to the stroke just described. The first fleet to have 'sevens' was that of Demetrius; it could well have been he, responsible for so many advances in the design of war galleys, who invented this type which involved a fundamental change from its predecessors.

Once the new method of rowing had been introduced, it must quickly have become apparent that there was no reason to stop at three men to the oar. Thus, alongside the 'four', which, as we suggested, was a beefed-up trireme, it was now possible to build a totally new version which had 65
one level of four-man oars. Such a version offered one great advantage: only the man at the head of each oar had to be a trained rower; the other three simply supplied muscle. This was why ships with three-man oars, four-man oars and so on right up to eight, were standard in the seventeenth and eighteenth century: the benches in those days were manned mostly by poor unfortunates who had fallen afoul of the law and been condemned to the galleys; it was pure luck if any had ever even been near the water. With the naval race between Demetrius and Ptolemy producing ever larger fleets made up of ever larger units, there was an ever larger need for rowers; it was far easier to fill that need if the qualification for the greater part of each crew was not experience but muscle alone.

Indeed, any sea-power troubled by a shortage of rowers must have welcomed these powerful one-level types of war galley. They were necessarily broad in beam to accommodate six or more rowers in a horizontal line, and that made them slower and less manoeuvrable than the slenderer types. But broader beam permitted a broader deck, and a broader deck permitted a greater number of marines than any slenderer type could carry; if they were able to get their grappling hooks into one and board, they could be certain of victory. When in 264 BC the Romans entered the First Punic War, the bitter conflict with Carthage that was fought mainly on the sea, they had to build a navy from scratch and fill the benches with whatever manpower was available to them, mostly men off the farms and the like. They built themselves a fleet of 'fives' and loaded aboard each a contingent of 120 legionaries; undoubtedly the ships were of the type with five men to the oar whose ample deck could accommodate so great a number of fighting men.

On the other hand, there were still navies that favoured the use of the ram, and they very likely preferred the multi-level versions of the 'four' and 'five', which, being slimmer and driven by seated rowers, provided the speed and manoeuvrability that ramming demanded. For example, the Rhodian navy in its heyday in the second and third century BC relied principally on 'fours' and was renowned for the skill in ramming that it achieved with them; the indications are that the type they used was a two-level galley with two men to the oar in each level. The Carthaginian fleet that faced Rome in the First Punic War had a fearsome reputation for skill in ramming, and its standard unit was the 'five'; almost certainly the slender three-level version was represented as well as the one-level.

The designers of galleys in the seventeenth and eighteenth centuries knew only the single-level galley and hence, as mentioned above, could never go past eight men to the oar, an 'eight' to use the ancient terminology. What, then, was the oarage of the 'nines', 'tens', 'elevens' and still greater craft we hear of? Ancient shipyards for centuries had been building galleys with two or three superimposed lines of oars. If we assume that, after the introduction of the galley with one level of multiple-rower sweeps, naval architects moved on to designing hulls that would accommodate two or three levels of such sweeps, we can explain almost all the oversize types. A 'nine', for example, could have been a two-level galley with five men to the oar in the upper level and four to the oar in the lower; or it might have been a three-level galley with three to the oar in each. Demetrius' great 'sixteen' may have had two levels with eight- 66
man sweeps in each, or three levels with sixteen men distributed among them, say six to the oar in the thranite level and five to the oar in the zygite and thalamite.

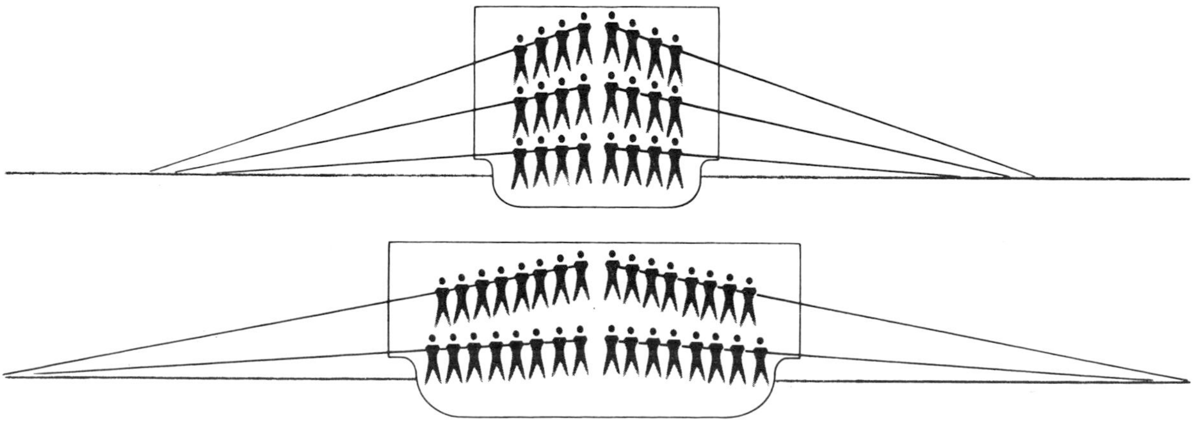

66 Possible arrangements of a 'twelve' and a 'sixteen'. The upper shows a three-level 'twelve', the lower a two-level 'sixteen'.

But what of Ptolemy II's 'thirty'? Even three levels of eight-man oars fall short of that figure. There is no question that the ship existed and, moreover, was prized, for the base of a statue has survived with an inscription in Greek reading 'King Ptolemy for Pyrgoteles, architect of the "thirty" and the "twenty"'; the statue that once stood on it had obviously been erected by a grateful monarch.

It is the monster 'forty' of Ptolemy IV that provides a vital clue. It was so extraordinary a work of man that the salient details about it were written down and thereby entered the historical record. Here they are, as reported by Athenaeus, a Greek writer of the second century AD who compiled a book given over to unusual matters of all kinds (the dimensions as cited by Athenaeus are in cubits, which I have converted to feet):

> It was 420 long, 57 from gangway to gangway, and 72 high to the prow ornament. From the stern ornament to the part where the ship entered the water was $79\frac{1}{2}$. It had four steering oars that were 45 long, and thranite oars – the longest aboard – that were 57; these, by virtue of having lead in the handles and being heavily weighted inboard, because of their balance were very easy to use. It was double-prowed and double-sterned.... During a trial run it took aboard over 4000 oarsmen and 400 other crewmen and, on the deck, 2850 marines.[2]

The mention of thranite oars implies the existence of zygite and thalamite; the ship, then, was a three-level galley. Now, if we try to distribute forty rowers over a thranite-zygite-thalamite triad, at least fourteen of the forty must be assigned to one oar, and the obvious candidate is the thranite, since we are specifically told that the thranite oars were the longest. But we are also told that they measured 57 feet (17.3 m), and a 57-foot oar is the proper size for only eight rowers, not fourteen. And what about the 2850 marines and 400 deckhands and the like? They must have been carried on the deck and, even if the deck of the 'forty' covered the whole expanse of the ship from the tip of the prow to the tip of the stern, it would still offer no more than some 24,000 square feet. This would have accommodated 3250 persons only if they were lined up as if on parade, leaving the deckhands no room in which to move about for handling lines and sail and the marines no room in which to take up a position for shooting arrows, hurling grapnels, etc.

The clue lies in the description of the vessel as 'double-prowed and double-sterned'. If it had two prows and two sterns, it must have been made up of two hulls yoked together – in other words, must have been what we call a catamaran. Now, if the hulls were not yoked close together but just far enough apart to allow for oarsmen on both the port and starboard side of each hull, we can explain why it was called a 'forty'.
Let us assume that there were eight men to each thranite oar, since that 67
is the proper number for a 57-foot oar. Assume seven men to each zygite oar and five to each thalamite. Each hull would thus be a 'twenty'; yoked together they make a 'forty'. We are told that there were four steering

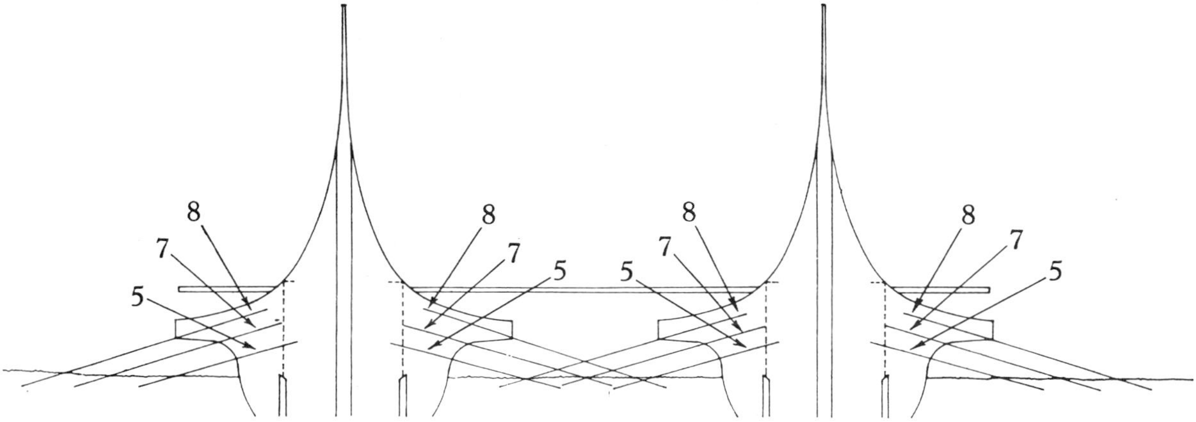

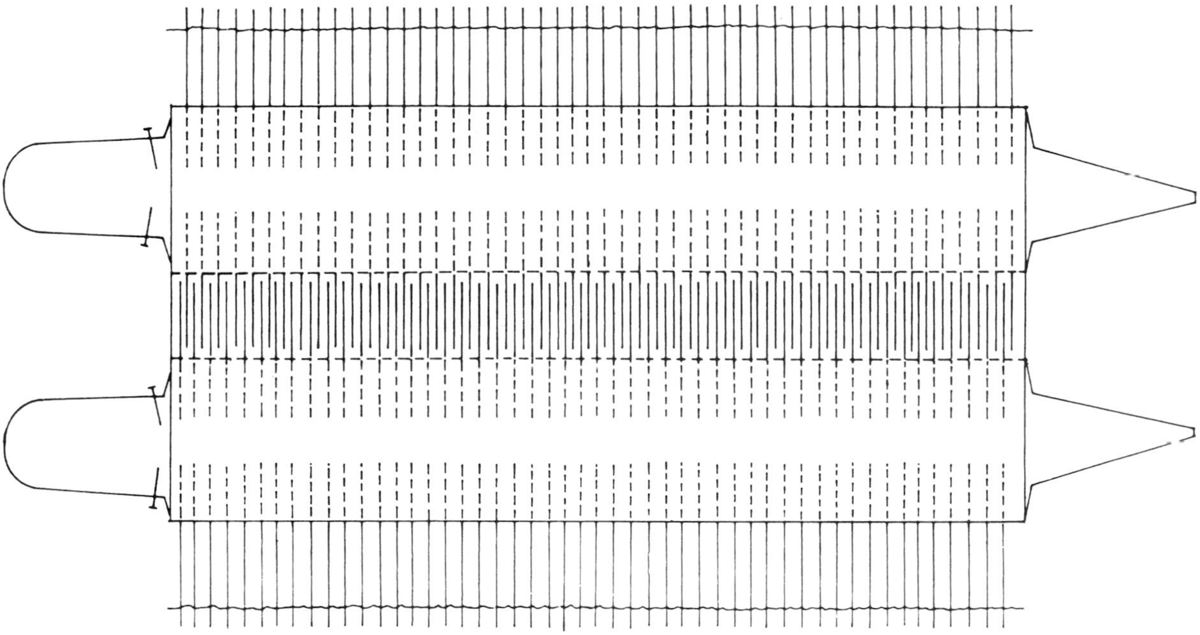

67 TOP Reconstruction of the 'forty' of Ptolemy IV viewed from the stern.

68 Reconstruction of the 'forty' viewed from above.

oars. This is what we should expect in a catamaran of such a size: to steer the unwieldy complex there was a steering oar on both the port and the starboard quarter of each hull. And the deck that spanned the twin 68
hulls, including the space between them, would be a vast affair, like the deck of an aircraft carrier, offering plenty of space for 400 deckhands and almost 3000 marines to carry out their duties. This monster of a ship was almost certainly not the first and only example of the catamaran galley. The 'thirty' of Ptolemy II that preceded it must have been a catamaran, made up of two 'fifteen' hulls yoked together. Very likely his 'twenty' was a catamaran as well.

We know the dimensions of the 'forty' only because they were unusual enough to be recorded; we have no information about those of any of the other types larger than a trireme. However, for one type, the one-level 'fives' used by the Romans in the First Punic War, we fortunately have grounds for a good guess. These ships, we happen to know, had a crew of 300. The figure includes officers, ratings and deckhands. On a trireme these numbered about fifteen; if for a 'five' we reckon on twenty or so, the total number of its oarsmen comes out to 280. At five to the oar, that works out to fifty-six oars, or twenty-eight to a side. In the late sixteenth century the French navy had galleys with almost the same oarage, twenty-six five-man oars a side. The ships were 180 ft 6 in. (55 m) long overall and had a maximum breadth of 26 ft 3 in. (8 m); the dimensions of the Roman one-level 'fives' could not have been very different.

In all the multi-rower galleys of the sixteenth to the eighteenth century, the oars were not worked over the gunwale but were housed in an oarbox which, instead of following the curve of the hull, had straight sides; in 44
bird's-eye view it looked like a long and narrow rectangular frame with the point of the vessel's prow emerging at one end and the bulge of its stern at the other. A similar arrangement was used for housing the multi-rower oars on Hellenistic galleys. In a mosaic of the first century BC, for 69
example, there appears a ship with just such a frame; protruding from it are two lines of oars set in echelon one slightly above the other. And a three-dimensional rendering of the front face of the oarbox forms part of the famous statue of the Victory of Samothrace, sculpted around 180 BC, which portrays the goddess of victory alighting on the prow of what is probably a Rhodian 'four'.

Although we cannot even guess at the dimensions of the galleys larger than a 'five', two recent archaeological finds provide dramatic proof of how monumentally big they must have been. We mentioned earlier (Chapter 6) the discovery in 1980 of a warship's ram off Athlit near 59, 6
Haïfa, a mighty sheath of high-grade bronze weighing 1023 pounds (465 kg). No remains of the vessel itself were found; the consensus at the time of discovery was that, to be equipped with so ponderous a weapon, it must surely have been one of the big types, perhaps even a 'ten'.

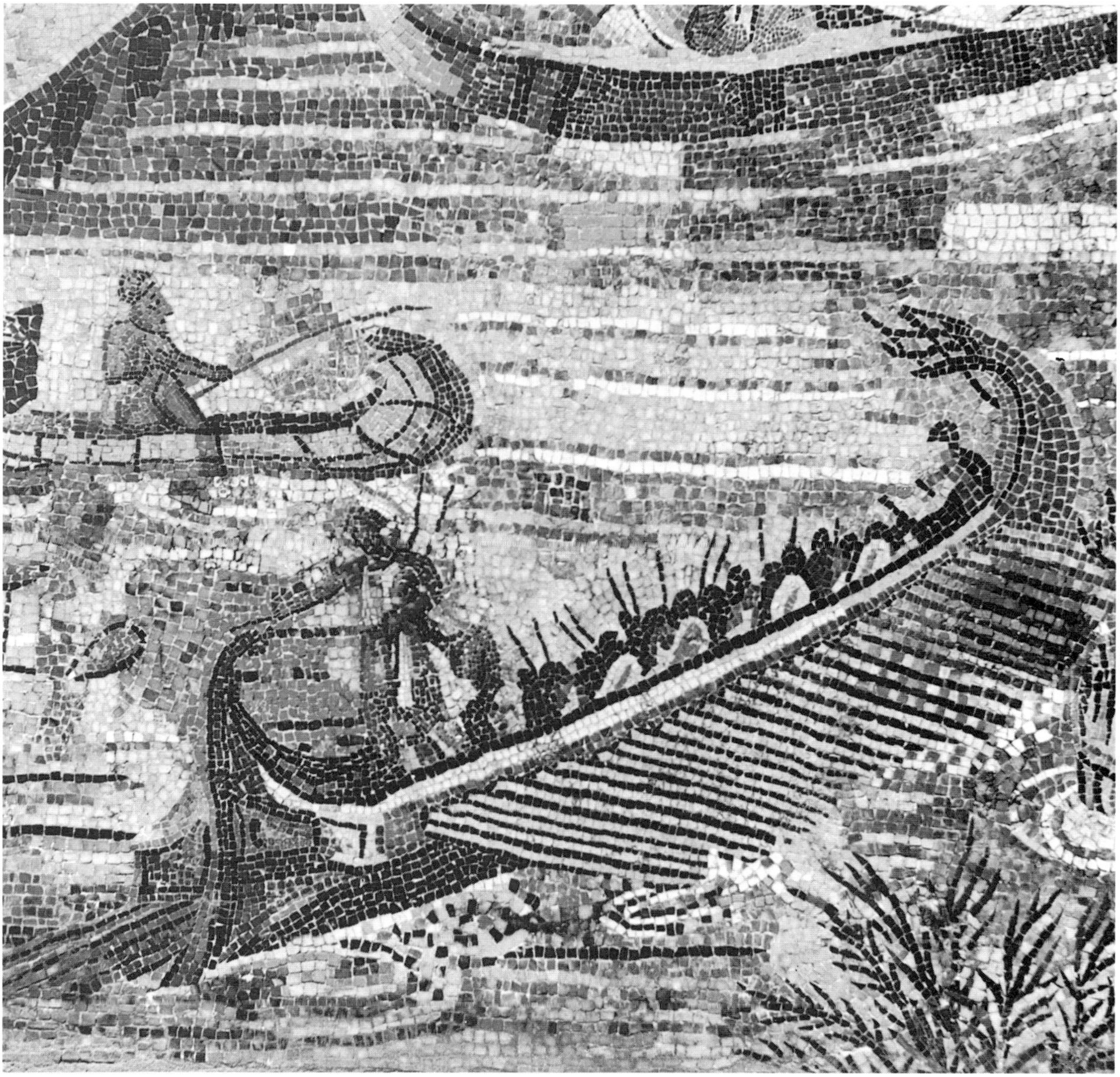

69 A two-level galley under way with a complement of marines on the deck. Both levels of oars work through an oarbox. Detail of a mosaic in the Palazzo Barberini at Palestrina, Italy. Early 1st century BC.

Then another archaeological discovery threw an entirely new light on the matter. In 31 BC Octavian – or Augustus, to give him the name he took later and by which he is better known – made himself sole ruler of Rome and its territories by defeating Mark Antony in a naval battle off Cape Actium. He commemorated the all-important victory by setting up in the neighbourhood an elaborate monument, one element of which was a display of rams taken from the ships that he had vanquished. Remains of the monument came to light in 1913. A number of years later it was noted that among its features was a line of curiously shaped sockets, diminishing in size, that had been cut into a long retaining wall. The reason for these remained a mystery until 1986, when it was observed 70
that their shape was just like the shape of the Athlit ram viewed head on. Their purpose now was clear: they held the rams that were part of the monument; they diminished in size because these were from galleys of

70 One of the sockets in Augustus' naval monument at Nicopolis. It held a ram somewhat bigger than the Athlit ram (Figs 59–60), perhaps from a 'six'. Late 1st century BC.

different sizes. We know that Antony had a heavy fleet ranging from triremes right up to 'tens'. The biggest sockets thus must have held the rams from 'tens' and the rest the rams from the various sizes below that. The striking fact is that, to judge from the size of the Athlit ram and the point in the series where this would place it, it came from at most a 'five', perhaps even a 'four'. The ram that went into the largest socket would have dwarfed it.

During the fourth century BC galleys grew in power and size, but rather slowly. The 'four' and the 'five' were introduced at the very beginning of the century, the 'six' sometime before the middle, but it was not until the third quarter that these sizes began to appear in fleets in significant numbers. Then, within less than half a century, there was a phenomenal increase from the 'six' to the 'thirty'. What caused it?

One obvious advantage of the bigger ships was that their greater expanse of deck space accommodated greater contingents of marines. This points to a change in the nature of naval battles; the age-old tactic of grappling and boarding had again come to the fore, and ramming no longer played as prominent a role as it had in the fifth and fourth centuries BC. The Athenian navy of that age, whose forte was the ram attack, had aboard each of its triremes no more than fourteen marines; the Romans in the First Punic War had aboard each of their one-level 'fives' one hundred and twenty. And a new piece of equipment was now added to aid the marines – wooden towers set up on the deck at prow and stern; 71
from the top of these, archers and javelineers could fire down on the enemy. The towers were collapsible so that they could be put in place just before a vessel went into action.

There was yet another reason for the increase in size: galleys now had to provide room for the mounting of catapults. The catapult was invented by the military engineers of Dionysius I around 400 BC for use in the besieging of walled cities. The earliest version was, in effect, an oversize bow mounted horizontally on a pedestal and fitted with a trough to hold a long arrow and with a windlass at the end of the trough to draw the bowstring. Within a few years a variation was devised that fired stone balls instead of arrows. By the middle of the fourth century a vastly more powerful form was developed, the torsion catapult, which could take much heavier darts or stone balls. Its drive was supplied not by a bow but by springs made up of tightly twisted skeins of sinew, cord or horsehair or even, in emergencies, women's hair.

Catapults were first used only on land. In 332 BC, when Alexander the Great was besieging the massively fortified Phoenician city of Tyre, he got the idea of mounting stone-throwing catapults on some of his second-class triremes – those rated as too slow for the line or those used for hauling troops – in order to pound the city's walls from the sea. Soon after, someone – it could well have been that imaginative military thinker,

71 A heavy two-level Roman warship. In the bows is a fighting tower. Marines preparing to leave the vessel line up behind a low parapet; two, in their eagerness, have already stepped over it. Relief found at Palestrina, Italy, and now in the Vatican Museum. Second half of the 1st century BC.

Demetrius – got the idea of putting catapults on his ships of the line to fire on enemy vessels. In 307 BC a great sea battle took place between Demetrius and Ptolemy I off the coast of Cyprus. Ptolemy's fleet had nothing bigger than 'fives'; Demetrius' had a good number of 'sixes' and 'sevens' as well as 'fives'. What is more, he had set up on his ships – no doubt the larger units but perhaps some of the smaller as well – both arrow-shooting and stone-shooting catapults; the arrow-shooting were of standard size, firing a dart 27 inches (68.5 cm) long. Eventually *katapeltaphetai* ('catapultists'), the ancient equivalent of naval gunners, became a fixed element in galley crews.

The shipboard catapults were probably mostly of the bow type, since it needed little maintenance and was unaffected by dampness, whereas torsion catapults needed constant care and their skeins were very sensitive to dampness. The darts and stones fired by the bow type would have served the purpose. A successful volley would have been quite enough to throw into disarray the marines on an enemy's deck, and, if a dart pierced the deck, it stood a good chance of hitting one or more of the rowers, causing a break in the stroke and an interruption in the vessel's advance. It has been reckoned that a one-level 'five' could accommodate ten standard arrow-shooting catapults and two stone-shooters capable of firing five-pound balls. There would be proportionately more catapults and of heavier calibre aboard bigger galleys; Demetrius' mighty 'sixteen' and Ptolemy II's mammoth 'twenty' and 'thirty' would have carried enough to lay down a veritable barrage.

Despite the increased emphasis on marines and the adding of catapults to a war galley's armament, ramming was by no means consigned to oblivion. All ships had rams, even the very largest, and they used them when they could. This is clear from the accounts of the naval battles of the time. One in particular is worth citing at length: written in a matter-of-fact style with no literary flourishes, it is the most detailed and trustworthy report we have of a fight in which big galleys, 'sevens' and up, took part. The author, Polybius, who wrote about half a century after it happened, had a professional knowledge of military matters and, as an important figure with friends in high places, had access to official records.

In 201 BC, off the island of Chios, the combined fleets of Pergamon and Rhodes attacked the fleet of Philip V of Macedon, last but one of the Antigonids. The battle opened with a drive by Attalus, king of Pergamon and in command of his country's contingent, against Philip's right wing. Here is Polybius' description of what then happened:

> Attalus' ship attacked an 'eight' and, getting its blow in first, struck it mortally below the waterline; although the marines on its deck kept on fighting for a long while, eventually he sank it. The flagship of Philip's fleet, a 'ten', fell into the enemy's hands in an unexpected fashion. A trireme-class galley came into its path and it rammed the vessel with a mighty blow amidships below the thranite oars; the ram, however, stuck fast, since the commander was not able to keep a check on his ship's impetus. So, with the vessel hanging from it, it was in a hopeless situation, utterly unable to move. At that moment two 'fives' fell on it and, wounding it fatally, one on each side, they destroyed the ship and all aboard, including Democrates, Philip's admiral. At the same time that this happened, Dionysodorus and Dinocrates, brothers and admirals on Attalus' side, launched attacks, one on an enemy 'seven' and the other on an 'eight', and suffered strange experiences in their combats. In his attack on an 'eight' Dinocrates' ship received a blow above the waterline, since the opposing vessel had its bows elevated, but struck the enemy below the waterline. At first he was unable to break free despite repeated attempts at backing water, and, since the Macedonian marines were fighting courageously, he was in the greatest danger. But Attalus came to his aid; by delivering a blow on the enemy ship he broke the embrace of the two vessels, and Dinocrates was in this unexpected way set free. The enemy marines all fought courageously but they were destroyed, and Attalus' men took over the undefended ship. Dionysodorus, charging with great force to deliver a blow, not only missed doing any harm but, being carried on past the enemy, lost his starboard oars, and the timbers supporting his towers were shattered. As soon as this happened enemy vessels surrounded him on all sides. Amid shouts and confusion the ship was destroyed with all aboard, except for Dionysodorus and two others who managed to swim to a small unit that came to their aid.[3]

The opponents were drawn up, as was customary, with the ships abreast in two long lines facing each other. When they came together, the fighting turned into a series of simultaneous individual encounters – and behind Polybius' matter-of-fact language we can discern the agonising drama that each of these represented. At one point along the line Attalus drove his ship against an 'eight' – we are never told the size of his ship but it must have been big to dare such an attack – and, by beating his opponent to the punch, delivered a fatal blow; as the stricken craft settled in the water, its marines desperately hurled missiles at Attalus' ship, which must have been warily standing by to make sure it went down. At another point along the line, Philip's flagship, a towering 'ten', rammed a trireme-class vessel; the blow from the massive beak reached up to the victim's topmost level of oars, but it had been delivered with too much drive, and the smaller vessel remained impaled on the ram. The attacker, so encumbered by the weight sticking to its bow that it could not move, became a defenceless target, and its crew watched horrified as one enemy 'five' bore down on it from port and another from starboard. At a third point, Dinocrates, attacking an 'eight', had the luck to hit it below the waterline since its bow was elevated – perhaps lifted by a wave or by its marines racing aft for some reason and depressing the stern – but he also struck too hard and, though the blow he gave it was mortal, his ram remained wedged in the hull; the crew frantically backed water to no avail, and he was miraculously saved when Attalus' big ship came up in the nick of time and drove into the 'eight' with such force that the ram was shaken loose. Attalus then swept the deck clear of the marines defending it, boarded, and took it as a prize – thereby sparing the lives of the hundreds manning the oars. In the other encounters few of the rowers could have escaped death, certainly none in the lowest levels.

The mammoth galleys of Demetrius and the Ptolemies were short-lived; they did not last much beyond the middle of the third century BC. But the classes just below them, from 'sevens' to 'tens', remained in the ranks right down to the Battle of Actium in 31 BC. That encounter, however, marked their end. For it left the victor, Augustus, in total control of the Mediterranean with no other fleet in existence to challenge him, and his successors continued to enjoy this state of affairs. Heavy combat units, in other words, had lost their reason for being.

Augustus refashioned the Roman navy, tailoring it to fit the new circumstances. Since it now had only peacetime duties to carry out – patrolling the coasts to hold down piracy, ferrying troops in an emergency, transporting government officials, and so on – he drastically reduced the size of its galleys. He created two major squadrons, the bigger and more important based near Naples, the smaller at Ravenna. The flagship of the first was a 'six', that of the other a 'five'; each had 72
some 'fours', but all the rest of their units were triremes plus a handful of liburnians, light and fast two-level galleys that were the ancient equivalent of destroyers. Minor squadrons were stationed at strategic points around the Mediterranean, and these consisted wholly of liburnians.

72 Ships of a Roman fleet commanded by the emperor Trajan approach a port. In the centre is the flagship, a three-level galley, probably a trireme, with its bowspritsail-like foresail raised. Above and below are two-level units, probably liburnians. Relief on the Column of Trajan, Rome. Early 2nd century AD.

Every galley still had a ram, but the shape was changed: it now ended in a blunt point instead of an oblong face with three transverse fins. The new form could hardly inflict the damage that the old was capable of, but that did not matter, since it was never called on to serve as a weapon. On the other hand, it was a good deal easier and cheaper to make and it continued to perform its important symbolic function as the badge of a warship.

In the third century AD, the Roman Empire was buffeted by political and economic disturbances from within and invasions of barbarians from without. Its once fine navy was allowed to decay. In the fourth century the triremes, liburnians and the other craft that had made up its squadrons vanished from the Mediterranean. The stage was set for their replacement by the very different galleys of the Byzantine Empire.

8

Winning with Fire: Warships of the Byzantine Navy

In AD 330 Constantine the Great shifted the capital of the Roman Empire from Rome to a new city named after himself, Constantinople, the modern Istanbul, planted on the site of the ancient Greek Byzantium. The previous century had been marked by almost constant turmoil, particularly in the western areas of the realm, and Constantine wanted the seat of his rule to be in the east, where he stood a greater chance of restoring order and stability. After his death the split between the eastern and the western parts deepened until, in AD 395, the empire was officially divided in two, each half with its own ruler. The western empire gradually fell into the hands of invaders – Goths, Franks, Vandals. But the eastern was of sterner stuff: the Byzantine Empire, as the nation that arose there is called, prospered and was strong enough to fight off its enemies right up to 1453 when the Turks gave it the *coup de grâce* with the capture of Constantinople. One of the reasons for its long life was sea power. It maintained a navy that, to the end of the first millennium, was supreme in the eastern Mediterranean. The ships of its fleet were not descended from those that had served the Roman Imperial navy. They were of different design and carried a new type of weapon.

Six years before moving to his new capital, Constantine had eliminated the last rival to the throne, Licinius. One of the major battles against him was fought on the sea, at the entrance to the Dardanelles. Licinius at the time was based in the east, and, by scouring the ports of Egypt, Asia Minor and the Levant, had managed to put together a fleet of 350 triremes. Constantine pitted against these a force consisting of 200 thirty-oared galleys and some fifty-oared. He won, and the victory sounded the death knell of the trireme. Naval architecture had come full circle: the galleys of the future were to be like those that had served Greeks and Phoenicians almost a thousand years earlier.

By the reign of Justinian in AD 527–65, the eastern empire had a formidable navy at its disposal. The ships resembled those with which Constantine had defeated Licinius; triremes and liburnians and the other craft of its predecessor were a thing of the past. The new craft were cataphract galleys but with only one level of rowers. They must have been lightly built, for their prime characteristic was their speed. It was reflected in the name they were given, *dromon* ('racer').

We are particularly well informed about the Byzantine navy of somewhat later times, around AD 900. This is because there has survived a handbook, drawn up by the emperor then on the throne, Leo VI 'The Wise' (886–912), that gives a succinct but detailed account of its ships, procedures, battle tactics and so on. It was a navy whose major units were much heavier and more dangerously armed than those Justinian had commanded.

The ships of the line in Leo's day, though still called *dromons*, had
two levels of oars with twenty-five in each level on each side, for a total 73

rowing contingent of 100 men. They were built in different sizes to accommodate more or fewer marines. The largest, the *dromon* in a strict sense, had a complement of at least 200 men. Fifty of these manned the lower level of oars; the rest manned the upper level, or served as marines, or did both, since it was assumed that, when the occasion required, upper-level rowers would drop their oars and take up weapons. The next smaller size, the *pamphylos*, had a complement of from 120 to 160. The smallest was called the *ousiakos* because it was manned by a single *ousia* or company of 100 men, to serve as rowers.

All three sizes were similar in build. They had a foredeck and afterdeck, gangways along each side and a catwalk down the middle, but were otherwise open. The *dromon* proper, to accommodate its greater number of marines, must have been longer than the others and with ampler decking fore and aft. To give the rowers some protection, a light frame was rigged along the gangways on which shields could be hung. There was no oarbox; both levels of oars were worked through ports in the hull. There was a raised platform forward for the fighting personnel and, on the big units, another amidships. The rig consisted of a mainmast and a foremast; the *dromon* proper may have had a mizzen as well. Very likely they carried lateen sails; these had been known since at least

73 A two-level *dromon*. Note that the vessel has no ram. Illustration from a manuscript in the Stadtbibliothek, Berne (Cod. Berne 120, fol. 119), 12th century AD.

74 Prow of a warship equipped with a fire-pot. A fighting tower stands in the bows and, at the end of a pole projecting from it over the prow, hangs a pot full of blazing fire. Graffito on the wall of a tomb in the Anfushi Necropolis, Alexandria, 1st century BC.

the second century AD (Chapter 9) and by the Middle Ages were to be the preferred type in the Mediterranean. The masts were not retractable; Byzantine galleys, unlike their predecessors, went into battle with masts upright and sails aboard.

Backing up the *dromons* were several types of light one-level craft. One of these, the *galea*, deserves mention, for it is the source of our word 'galley'. The chroniclers and historians of the Middle Ages for some reason chose it as a term for oared vessels in general, and English took it over with that meaning.

What set the Byzantine ships of the line apart from all their predecessors was their major weapon – fire. Soon after the beginning of the seventh century the Byzantine Empire found a new and dangerous enemy across the water, the Arabs. In AD 636 the Arabs had embarked upon their spectacular career of conquest by seizing Syria and, shortly thereafter, Egypt. With the ships and shipyards of the Levant and Alexandria in their hands, they were able to put together a powerful navy and, in 673, they sent off a formidable armada to besiege and take Constantinople. Year after year they launched furious assaults, but were repulsed every time until finally, in 679, they gave up and sailed home.

Constantinople owed its salvation to a timely invention by a Greek engineer named Callinicus, a refugee who had fled there when the Arabs overran his home town in Syria. Fire had long been used in warfare in one way or another. On land, archers would at times shoot arrows swathed in cloth that had been soaked in an inflammable mixture and ignited. On the sea, the Rhodian navy had once won some timely victories by hanging pots of blazing fire over the bows of their galleys. 74
The mixtures, later known as 'Greek fire', usually had as their principal ingredient naphtha, as the ancients called crude oil, which, throughout the oil-rich areas of the Near East, could be scooped up at dozens of points where it seeped out of the ground. Although it was inflammable enough in its natural state, it was common practice to lace it with sulphur or pitch or quicklime. Then came a revolutionary discovery: if saltpetre were added, a mixture resulted that was capable of spontaneous combustion. Callinicus may have been the one who hit on this, or he may have been the one who perfected the mechanism that made it possible to use Greek fire so effectively on shipboard. It not only saved Constantinople but supplied the Byzantine navy with its chief weapon for the future; by keeping it a secret from its opponents, it was able to hold a clean advantage over them for centuries.

The *dromons* were designed and equipped for fighting at close quarters, and their prime weapon was Greek fire. Each, states Leo,

> is to have forward in the bows its *siphon*, sheathed with bronze as is customary, by means of which the fire that has been prepared will be discharged upon the enemy. Above the *siphon* will be a platform of planks with an encircling railing of planks where marines will be stationed.[1]

75 A ship of the fleet of the Byzantine emperor Michael II (AD 820–9) envelops an enemy with fire from a *siphon* set in the bow. The caption reads: 'The fleet of the Romans pouring fire on the fleet of the enemy.' The ship carries a lateen sail. Illustration from a manuscript of Iannes Scylitzes, 14th century AD, in the Biblioteca Nacional, Madrid.

This *siphon* that was to nestle in the eye of the ship under the forward fighting platform was the ancient version of a flame thrower. It consisted of a cannon-like tube of wood lined with bronze, to the inboard end of 75
which was fitted a vessel containing the Greek fire; somehow this was forced up to the muzzle of the tube – perhaps it was heated by a brazier underneath the vessel and put under pressure by an air pump attached to the vessel – and, as it emerged, a marine stationed near the muzzle touched a torch to it, causing it to belch into a sheet of flame. The largest *dromons* mounted a *siphon* amidships and aft as well as forward. The *siphon* was the most important fire weapon. But, in addition, there were catapults which shot not only missiles as their predecessors had, but also grenades, pots of Greek fire that would explode on impact.

The *dromons* were fitted with rams, as war galleys had been for almost two millennia. But, since the aim now was to get close to the enemy and grapple, the ram was not a primary weapon. Ships no longer opened an attack, as triremes and the other types of war galley of the past had, by manoeuvring to deal a mortal blow with it. The ram now aided in fighting at close quarters or helped to finish off a wounded opponent. Leo, for example, explains how

> it is possible to destroy an enemy vessel as follows. One *dromon* comes alongside and grapples it; the enemy, as is their way, will run together to the side where the hand to hand fighting is taking place, with the aim of resting their own ship against the *dromon*. At this point another *dromon* will drive against the side of the enemy vessel near the stern and, in the collision, give

that side a hard push. The first *dromon*, loosing itself from its lashings, can back off a bit so that the enemy vessel will not be leaning on it, and the other *dromon* will then hit the enemy with full force, totally destroying the vessel with every man aboard.[2]

Leo is emphasising the advantage of having *dromons* operate in pairs. One closes in and grapples, getting the enemy marines to rush over to the side being attacked and thereby causing their vessel to list. At this point a second *dromon* delivers a stroke of the ram, which will shove the enemy craft over still further. Then the first casts off and backs away; its team-mate, before the enemy marines have time to rush to their original stations and bring their ship back to its proper trim, lands a blow on the tilted side which, piercing it on the waterline or below, will be fatal.

The surviving representations of Byzantine galleys all date from later times when the ram had disappeared, so we have no idea of its shape. Most likely it was single-pointed, as on the galleys of the Roman Empire, since its function was secondary and this form was easier and cheaper to make.

From about AD 1000 onward, the enemies of the Byzantine Empire grew ever stronger at its expense. The states of the west, notably Venice, steadily weakened its control of the sea. In the east the Turks unrelentingly seized more and more of its territory; their gradual annexation, from the eleventh century on, of Asia Minor cut off a key source of wealth. The emperors, some without the resources to maintain the fleet and others without the interest, allowed it to decay; by the fourteenth century it was down to a mere handful of units.

The ancient war galley had finally come to the end of its long life. The stage was set for the début of its medieval descendants.

9

Merchantmen

At a marina in Piraeus, Athens' port today as in ancient times, there is a dock where passers-by are astonished to see, in the line of sleek yachts, a boat that looks as out of place as a Roman chariot amid a batch of motor cars. It is a replica of a small coastal vessel of about 300 BC. This ancient craft was a merchantman and, as we shall see, owes its resurrection to the cargo it was carrying, a load of jars of wine.

Maritime commerce played a major role in the economy of Greece and Rome. Greek cities, as we have already remarked, started as small independent states consisting of an urban centre with a certain amount of territory surrounding it. As time passed, some of the centres grew so big that they had too many mouths to feed from the grain raised locally. At first they met the problem by creaming off the excess mouths and sending them to found colonies all around the Mediterranean and Black Sea, a movement that went on from about 700 to 500 BC. Inevitably the problem returned, and, since most of the feasible sites had already been colonised, the city-states, reluctantly abandoning the ideal of self-sufficiency, turned to importing the grain they needed. They drew supplies from south Russia, whose rich soil, then as now, produced abundant crops, far in excess of what was consumed by its population. They drew from Egypt as well, where the fields along the Nile, irrigated by its annual flood, also yielded a sizeable surplus. During the Hellenistic Age, with the increase in the size of states and their capitals, the amount of grain that crossed the water increased in proportion. During the centuries of Roman Imperial rule that followed, the volume grew steadily larger, with north Africa joining in as a major supplier. Grain was to the ancient world what oil is to ours: from the sixth century BC up to its end, the Mediterranean and Black Sea were studded with vessels, great and small, hauling this vital import.

Two other commodities were close runners-up to grain in ancient international trade, wine and olive oil. Wine was far more important then than now: for Greeks and Romans it took the place of coffee, tea, soft drinks, juices, and so on, as well as serving as an accompaniment to food. Cnidus, on the south-west coast of Asia Minor, and Rhodes, just off it, sent shiploads of *vin ordinaire* to Athens, Alexandria and other centres where the demand was too great to be satisfied by the local vineyards. The cargoes could run to great size, at times many thousands of jars. Some shippers, to avoid dealing with a hold full of a multitude of such jars, used an ancient version of the tanker, a ship whose hold was fitted permanently with *dolia*, mammoth containers made of clay that were often some 6 feet (2 m) in height and diameter, weighed a ton empty, and had a capacity of up to 800 gallons (4000 l).

Fine wines were produced in many places, on the islands of Lesbos, Samos and Chios off Asia Minor, on the island of Thasos in the north Aegean, in parts of Italy, and elsewhere. They too were exported in large quantities. Demosthenes, who gained his fame as a public speaker but earned his living as a lawyer, once represented a client in a case involving a vessel that was to load aboard 3000 jars from Mende in northern Greece, which produced a prized wine, and carry them to the Crimea, where there was a clutch of Greek cities and where the shippers could count on a return cargo of south Russian grain.

Olive oil, too, was far more important in the daily life of the ancients than it is today. It served the purposes that butter, soap and electricity serve for us: they cooked with it, cleansed themselves with it, and burned it as fuel in their lamps. The Greeks who had settled on the shores of the Black Sea, where the olive does not grow, imported it from Greece and Asia Minor. Rome, with its enormous population to take care of, brought in huge amounts from north Africa and Spain.

A pair of items that also bulked a good deal larger then than now in international commerce was salt-fish and what the Romans called *garum*, a fish sauce that seems to have been close kin to the types widely used today in the Far East; it was made by allowing heavily salted chunks of fish to ferment and drawing off the liquid that formed. Both rich and poor spiced their food with *garum*, and it came in a whole series of grades to satisfy the tastes of its varied customers. The Black Sea was the chief supplier for the eastern portion of the Mediterranean world, Spain for the western.

Grain, wine, olive oil, salt-fish, *garum* – hauling principally these but also numerous other items for long and short distances kept merchantmen of all sizes moving along the coasts or crossing the open waters of the Mediterranean and Black Sea. For a long time we knew of the ships that did the carrying only at second hand, through remarks made by Greek and Roman writers, terse mentions in documents, representations in painting or sculpture or on coins. Then, as we noted earlier (Chapter 3), around the middle of this century the discoveries of marine archaeologists opened an entirely new chapter in ancient maritime history; now, thanks to the examination of wrecks, we have first-hand knowledge of what ancient merchantmen were like – not all of them, unfortunately, chiefly those that had cargoes of wine or olive oil or *garum*. This is because these products were transported in containers of clay.

The ancient equivalent of our barrel or steel drum was the amphora, a distinctive type of big jar. Etymologically the name means 'carried on both sides'; amphoras were so called because they had a pair of handles set vertically opposite one another near the rim. From a relatively narrow mouth and neck they bulged out into a more or less cylindrical body and then tapered to end in a point. They generally stood some 3 feet high (1 m) and held between 5 and 10 gallons; a very common size was just under 7 gallons (26 l). Being thick-walled, they were heavy: the 7-gallon size, for example, weighed some 50 pounds empty (approx. 26 kg) and double that when full; stevedores could handle only one at a time balanced 76

76 Stevedores unloading a cargo of amphoras. A checking clerk sits in front of a table with an open ledger on it. Two assistants stand to his right. As each stevedore comes down the gangplank shouldering an amphora, he receives a tally-piece from one of the assistants, while the clerk makes an appropriate entry in the ledger. The stevedore will presumably turn in his tally-pieces at the end of the day and be paid according to the number he has amassed. Relief found at Portus and now in the Torlonia Museum, Rome; 3rd century AD.

on the shoulder. They were sealed with stoppers of fired clay or, less often, of cork, usually set in mortar.

Amphoras differed according to time and place. Each region made them in a different shape and, as time passed, certain features tended to change: the curve of the lip or of the handles would vary, the neck would grow longer or shorter, the body narrower or fuller, and so on. Moreover, the handles often bore, stamped on them, the symbol of the place of origin or the name of the shipper. As a result, these humble containers, which have about as much aesthetic appeal as a barrel, are archaeological treasures: from the general shape excavators can determine where an amphora came from, just as we can distinguish a bottle of Burgundy wine from one of Bordeaux, and from the individual characteristics they can tell to what century, sometimes even to what half-century, it belongs. From the names of the shippers we can even at times trace the exact point of origin. And, when amphoras make up the cargo of a ship, they not only provide these indications of route and date but perform another invaluable service: they often preserve from deterioration or destruction the part of the hull over which they lie. 77

When an ancient vessel came to grief and landed on the sea floor, the movement of water and sand and the action of marine borers gradually

77 Amphoras of various shapes and sizes from wrecks found off the Grand Congloué island near Marseilles. Early 2nd century BC.

destroyed the exposed parts of the hull and other elements made of organic matter. This is why no hulls of sunken war galleys are ever found: their bronze fittings can last but everything else, being of wood, will disappear. This is also why no hulls of freighters carrying grain are ever found: grain was transported in bulk or in sacks, and if a ship loaded with it went to the bottom, the cargo soon vanished along with the hull. Clay, however, is well-nigh indestructible. Thus when a vessel laden with amphoras of wine or oil or *garum* went down, after its rigging, spars, decks, and the sides of the hull had been eroded away, there would be laid bare the cargo of jars inside, lying in a heap to flag forever the presence of an ancient ship. This is why so many of the wrecks that the divers have found turn out to be of freighters filled with amphoras.

In order to avoid breakage ancient stevedores stowed the amphoras in the hold with extreme care. The jars were set upright in superimposed tiers, each jar being so placed that its pointed bottom would fit into the 22
open space around the necks of those in the tier below; on big merchantmen carrying thousands of jars there could be as many as five tiers. Dunnage of twigs and branches cushioned the jars against each other and the lowest tier against the bottom of the hold. When marine archaeologists began excavating such wrecks and removing the amphoras, they made the gratifying discovery that very often this tightly woven mass of jars

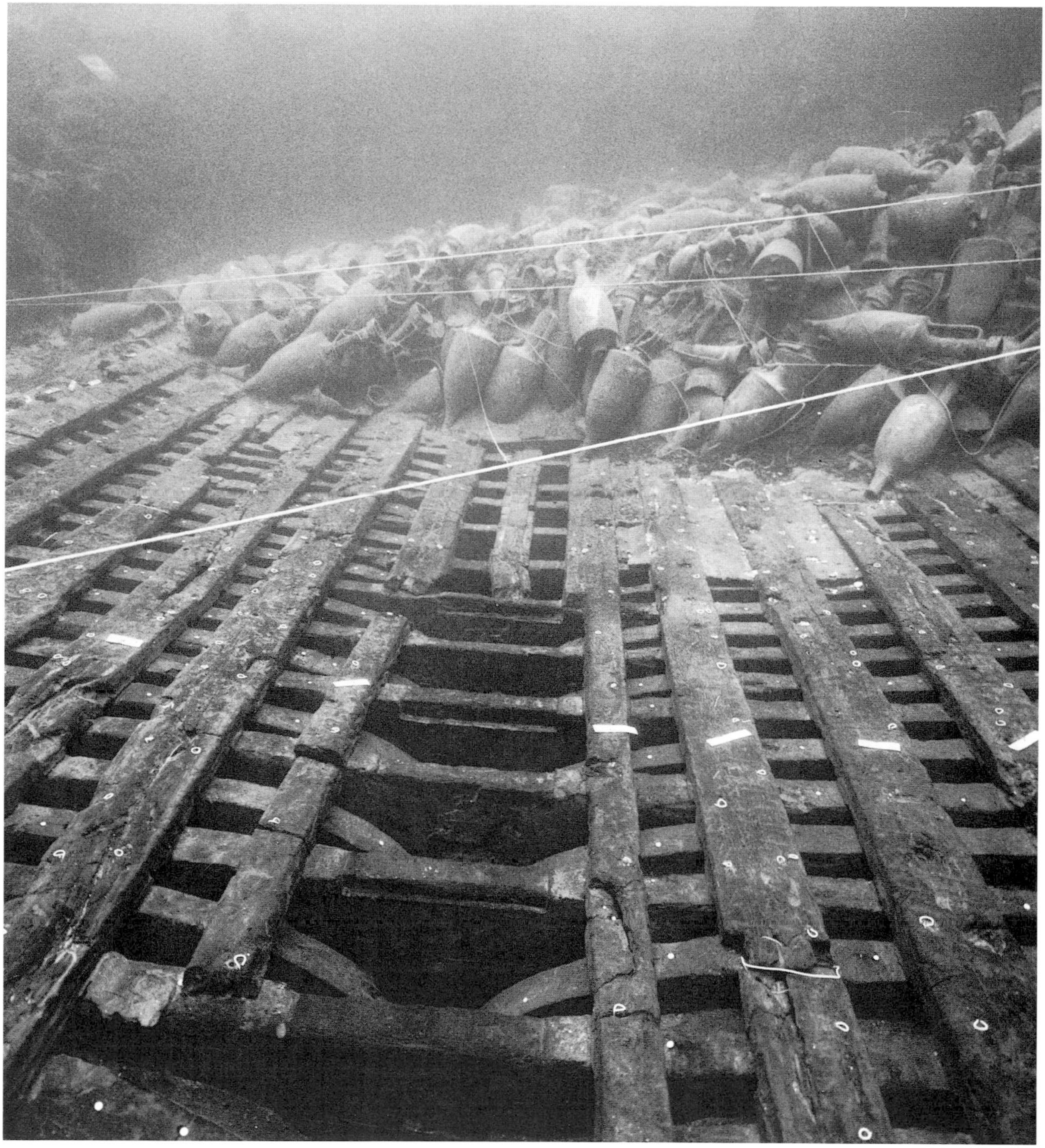

78 The removal of part of the cargo of amphoras from the wreck, found at La Madrague de Giens off Toulon, of a big Roman merchantman – about 130 feet (40 m) long with a capacity of perhaps 400 tons – revealed that the wood underneath was perfectly preserved. Visible are the line of frames, consisting of alternate floor timbers that cross the whole bottom of the vessel and half frames that curve up from either side of the keel and run over the bottom on either side, and the ceiling, the long timbers that run fore and aft over the frames. The white circles mark the nails that hold the ceiling to the frames, and the white dots mark the treenails that hold the frames to the planking; the planking is equally well preserved. Mid-1st century BC.

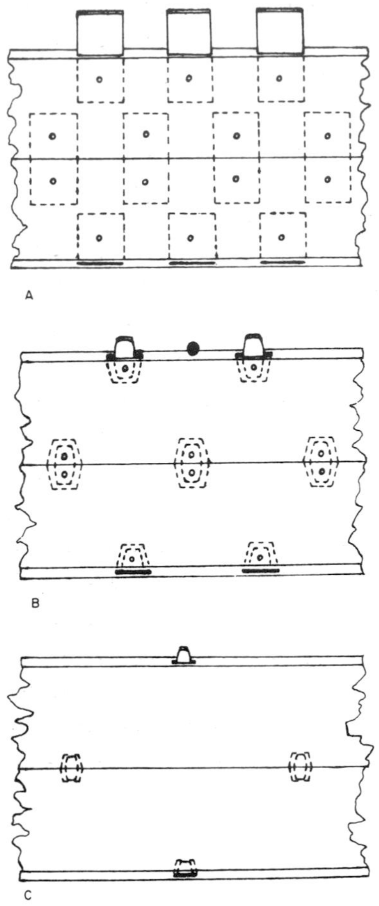

79 Diagrams illustrating the changes in the nature of mortises and tenons over the centuries: (A) mortises and tenons typical of wrecks dating up to the 1st century AD; (B) mortises and tenons found in a wreck of the 4th century AD; they are smaller, placed further apart, and the tenons fit loosely instead of snugly in the mortises; (C) mortises and tenons found in a wreck of the 7th century AD; they are even smaller and are set even further apart, the tenons fit loosely in the mortises, and they are no longer locked in place by transfixing dowels.

had saved from destruction the part of the hull underneath it, in some instances so efficiently that the wood was practically in mint condition 78
(see Chapter 3). In the case of a small vessel that had sunk around 300 BC off the town of Kyrenia on the north coast of Cyprus, the load of 400 jars had preserved so much of the hull that its discoverers were able to build the full-scale replica mentioned at the outset of this chapter. As we noted in Chapter 3, study of such remains has revealed that the ancient Mediterranean shipwrights had their own special way of putting together a hull: they built up a shell of planking by joining planks edge to edge 24–7
with closely set mortise and tenon joints, each transfixed by dowels above and below the seam to keep it locked in place, and then into this shell they inserted framing. The result was a hull that was strong and staunch and needed no caulking; indeed, there was no room to insert any in the seams, crossed as these were by a continuous line of tenons. However, the method was costly. Not only did it require long hours of labour to rough out the shape of the planks and insert and fit the innumerable joints, but it was prodigal in its use of material. For the planks had to be more or less carved out into their ultimate shape; it has been estimated that on some hulls as much as seventy per cent of the raw timber might be cut away as waste.

As time went on, this inescapable economic fact had its impact. Of the hulls that have survived, the greatest number range in date from the fourth century BC onward. They show that, down to the first century BC, shipwrights concentrated on the shell of planking: they made the mortise and tenon joints large, set them so closely that sometimes there is hardly any space between, fitted them tightly, and transfixed them with dowels. 25–6
Sometimes they even gave the shell two layers of planking, each carefully 29
joined with mortises and tenons. At times, particularly on big hulls, they covered the underwater surface with a sheathing of thin lead plates laid 91,
over a lining of fabric impregnated with pitch or resin to protect the 105,
wood against attack by shipworms, which thrive in the warm waters of the Mediterranean (sheathing a vessel in this way went out of practice at the end of the ancient world and was not revived until the eighteenth century). But, from the first century AD onwards, shipwrights began to introduce procedures that clearly would have had the effect of reducing costs. They made the mortise and tenon joints smaller, allowed them to 79
fit more loosely, and, by spacing them further apart, cut down the number. To compensate, they strengthened the internal structure. For example, they increasingly adopted the practice of fastening at least some of the frames to the keel, thereby converting this into a veritable backbone for the hull. A wreck of the seventh century AD discovered near Yassi Ada, a tiny island off the south-west coast of Asia Minor, reveals that by this time shipwrights were on their way toward the assembling of a hull in the manner that was to be standard in Europe from the Middle Ages on, in which a skeleton of keel and frames is first set up and a skin of

planking is then fastened to it. In this wreck the shell of planks had been put together in minimal fashion: the joints are very small, are set far apart, and are very loose, with the mortises being far bigger than the tenons, and they lack the transfixing dowels. What is more, after building up the shell as far as the waterline, the shipwright changed his procedure: at that point he inserted frames and simply nailed the rest of the planking to these. By the end of the first millennium AD the last step had been taken. The proof is provided by a wreck discovered a little further to the south, off Serçe Liman on the coast of Asia Minor facing the northern part of Rhodes. The hull of this ship, which went down about AD 1025, had been totally built skeleton-first.

At times the indestructibility of clay preserves even more than the bare hull. In the Yassi Ada wreck just mentioned, the excavators came upon some clay tiles, and these enabled them to reconstruct the ship's galley. The tiles, it was clear, had belonged to the roof of some compartment and, when the wooden structure they sat on was eaten away and collapsed, they had fallen to the floor. The excavators, by carefully noting and analysing their location, were able to determine the compartment's approximate dimensions, about 11 by 4 feet (3.3 × 1.2 m); they estimated the headroom at 6 feet (1.8 m). The discovery of cooking utensils all around, plus other tiles in the area which turned out to come from a firebox, identified the area as the galley. Remains of some iron bars 80

80 Reconstruction of the galley of the Yassi Ada wreck (7th century AD). On the floor is a firebox made of clay tiles which was probably topped by a grid of iron bars.

nearby showed that the firebox was topped by a grill. Since the vessel was just a small freighter some 70 feet (21 m) long, such a galley was a surprisingly ample facility, far more, for example, than Columbus' ships boasted (all they had was a wooden firebox, its bottom covered by a bed of sand, tucked under the forecastle and shielded from the wind by a hood).

In the case of the Kyrenia wreck, the overlay of amphoras enabled its discoverers to conclude that the vessel, a small freighter about 45 feet (13.7 m) long, had only four hands in its crew, and that they did without the convenience of a galley. In the forward area, where the water cask was customarily placed, the excavators found four identical cups, and, in the after area, where gear was customarily stored, they found four wooden spoons and four oil jugs plus a whole array of utensils connected with food – a copper cauldron, clay cooking pots, plates, bowls, jugs. There was, however, no sign of a firebox or anything like it. Very likely this little vessel tramped along the coast and, when it was time to eat, put in and let the men cook ashore.

Amphoras that were stowed amidships can preserve two other key features of a hull, the mast-step and the well for collecting bilge-water. The mast-step is generally a long timber, with a socket for receiving the 81
heel of the mast, which overlies a good part of the keel, thereby distributing the strain caused by the working of the mast; on big ships this timber is massive as well as long. Sometimes the divers discover a coin in the socket; it was placed there for good luck when the ship was launched, a custom that has lasted to this day. Such a discovery is certainly a piece of luck for the marine archaeologist, for it means that the vessel was built while the coin was in circulation, and that can usually be determined, often with precision. The well for collecting bilge-water is a box-like chamber in the deepest part of the hull. Around it are frequently found fragments of lead tubing, which, together with other indications, make it certain that ships had pumps to empty out the water collected there.

81 The mast-step of the Madrague de Giens wreck (see Fig. 78). The large cavity received the heel of the mast. The other cavities were for the elements of the mast-case which embraced the lowermost part of the mast.

How the hulls of ancient merchantmen were built, what fittings they had, what cargo was put into the hold and how it was stowed, even how hulls were repaired and how long they could last (the Kyrenia wreck seems to have been some eighty years old when it went down, and had undergone numerous repairs) – on all this marine archaeology has shed totally new light. But for the other features of ancient merchantmen, their superstructure, deck fittings, rig, and the like, the most important sources of information, with a few exceptions, are the representations that have survived.

There must have been sailing ships of as many different shapes and rig in antiquity as there are now. The representations available, however, being mostly small, often crude, and never to scale, permit us to detect only the most obvious distinctions. The most striking of them is in the

shape of the prow. Usually it is more or less rounded, the form we are familiar with. But many vessels, running the gamut of size from mere row-boats to large seagoing freighters, have an unfamiliar type of prow, one that is concave in profile and at the waterline ends in a jutting cutwater very much like the ram of a war galley. Such a prow is generally 82
accompanied by a curved figurehead in the form of a scroll or similar ornament. Of the vessels with traditional prows, one variety, with a hull so very rounded that it is almost crescent-shaped, has but a simple upright stempost with no figurehead; it is sometimes just as plain aft, but 84
sometimes adorned with a goose-headed sternpost. Another variety, marked by a distinctly heavier hull with less rounded lines, has a stempost that is capped by a massive block-shaped adornment. 85

On either side of the stempost was a carved device representing the ship's name. And far aft was the *tutela*, as it was called in Latin, the image 84
of the ship's guardian deity. This was so important that, on richly decorated craft, it might be gilded or even made of ivory. Ships were generally named after deities, especially those favoured by sailors, such

82 Two large Roman sailing vessels passing each other at the lighthouse marking the entrance to Portus, Rome's harbour. The ship to the right has the traditional rounded prow, while the ship to the left has a prow that ends at the waterline in a jutting cutwater much like the ram of a warship; its stempost is finished off with an adornment in the form of a scroll. Note its three masts; it carries a mizzen as well as main and foresail. The mosaic decorated the floor outside an office which, as the inscription reveals, belonged to 'the shippers of Sullecthum', a town on the eastern coast of Tunisia. Foro delle Corporazioni, Ostia. About AD 200.

83 The stern of a large sailing vessel in the act of leaving port. The ship is gaily decorated: part of the hull is painted dark red, the goose-necked sternpost is white with dark red stripes, the rail around the stern gallery is gilded, and there is a bright red stern patch. Mosaic found in a house in Rome and now in the Antiquarium of the Capitoline Museum. About AD 200.

as Isis and the Dioscuri (Castor and Pollux). Asklepios, the god of healing, was also popular; presumably he would keep a vessel sound. The name and guardian deity might be the same or might be different.
84 Vessels had aboard a portable altar to set up and use for offering sacrifice upon safe arrival or other occasions when divine aid was thanked or sought.

Representations show a deckhouse aft. Often it has a flat roof that serves as a sort of poop deck. Big ships were fitted with an overhanging gallery girdling the stern. On some the overhang is great enough to
83–4 supply space for a small shelter suspended over open water behind the sternpost; to judge from its position, this was probably a latrine. Between the deckhouse and the sternpost was where the helmsman generally took
84 his stand, gripping the inboard ends of the long tiller bars that led to the steering oar on each quarter. In the representations these look as if they would be difficult to handle, but apparently this was not the case. The Roman essayist Lucian, describing a big freighter he once saw, remarks that the ship 'all depended for its safety on one little man, already a greybeard, who turned those great steering oars with just a skinny tiller.'[1]

As we noted earlier (Chapter 4), the standard rig in antiquity was the square rig. A large square sail set amidships supplied most of the drive;
82–5 in the great majority of the representations it dwarfs the rest of the canvas. On big freighters whose routing took them regularly over open water, it was so broad as to require a yard nearly as long as the ship; when squared, its arms might reach so far beyond the hull that they could be fitted for dropping stones or other heavy weights on enemy vessels that came alongside in an attack. Multiple lifts – lines from the yard to the mast

84 OVERLEAF A big Roman merchantman depicted first as it sails past the lighthouse at the entrance to Portus, Rome's harbour, and then moored at a quay there. On the left, the ship is shown moving under topsail and shortened mainsail. The foresail has been lowered and stowed away, and a deckhand has rigged a bulky timber to the foresail halyard that will serve as a bumper when the vessel nears the quay. A hand in the ship's boat, which had been towed behind, is pulling it alongside. On the poop two men and a woman, probably the captain and a distinguished passenger and his wife, gather about an altar to make a thank-offering for their safe arrival. On the right, the ship is moored, prow to, by a line fastened to a stone ring jutting out from the quay. The topsail has been stowed away; the mainsail has been completely brailed up, and hands have gone aloft to secure it. Unloading has begun: a gangplank has been run from the bow rail to the quay, and on it is a stevedore hauling an amphora. Relief found at Portus and now in the Torlonia Museum, Rome. About AD 200.

V
L

50
3-4
32.

85 LEFT A sailing vessel entering port. One crewman, standing in front of the helmsman, has gathered the brails in his hand and is hauling on them. Two men are already aloft to secure the sail once it has been brailed up, and two are on their way; one uses the rope ladder on the after side of the mast and the other hauls himself up on the forestay. Relief on the tomb of Naevoleia Tyche, Pompeii. Mid-1st century AD.

86 BELOW LEFT This Roman sailing craft has a foresail that is almost as big as the mainsail. The foremast rakes forward in the traditional fashion. Relief found at Utica and now in the British Museum. About AD 200.

87 ABOVE In this vessel, pictured on a coin of Diocletian and Maximian that dates from AD 306, the foresail is not only as big as the mainsail but the foremast is almost vertical.

above – were needed to support it. The mast was stayed forward by a
massive forestay running from a point near the top of the mast to the 84
prow and laterally by shrouds that were set up with tackles so that they
could be adjusted; since shrouds so set up do not permit the fastening to
them of ratlines to serve as steps for getting aloft, there was a rope ladder 85
abaft the mast, a feature that would continue to mark Mediterranean
sailing craft during the Middle Ages and even later. Canvas was shortened, as it had been since at least the sixth century BC (see Chapter 4),
by brails. Pennants, probably for identification, were flown from the tip
of the mast or the yard-arms, and banners suspended from horizontal 83
staffs were displayed aft.

Most freighters were two-masters, carrying a foresail in addition to the
mainsail just described. When the foresail first appears, it is rather large,
perhaps half the size of the main, set on a foremast with a distinctly 38
forward rake (see Chapter 4). By the first century AD – perhaps even
earlier, but depictions are lacking so we cannot be sure – it had developed
in two directions. On most ships it had become a headsail pure and
simple, very much like the bowspritsail of later ages, a small rectangle of 76, 82, 84
canvas on a mast slanting over the bows. On some, however, it remained
as it had been five centuries earlier, a sail of fair size hung on a mast 86
almost as high as the mainmast. The foremast did not lose its forward
rake until close to the beginning of the fourth century AD, when it was
sometimes stepped almost upright. 87

On the bigger ships used for crossing open water, the mainsail's drive
was increased by the addition of a topsail, a small piece of canvas in the 82, 84
shape of a flattened isosceles triangle; the base was bent to the yard and
the apex to the tip of the mast. On the very biggest freighters, drive was
further increased by the addition of a mizzen hoisted on a short mast set 82
midway between the mainmast and the sternpost. Like the mainsail, the foresail and mizzen were fitted with brails for reefing. The continued use of this effective, safe and convenient way of shortening sail throughout antiquity was possible because the ancients, save for the handkerchief-sized topsail, never developed, as later ages did, the system of superimposing sails on a mast, a system that would have made them give up, at least for the upper tiers, the use of brails. The limiting of the spread of canvas to, at most, foresail, mainsail, main topsail and mizzen made for safe sailing but very slow speed. The fastest voyage on record in ancient times, from the Strait of Messina to Alexandria in six days, works out to an average of just under six knots; the crack sailing ships of the nineteenth century, spreading multiple levels of sail, were capable of runs that trebled that figure.

For a long time it was believed that the ancients did not know the fore-and-aft rig, that is, the type of rig in which the sail, instead of being set so that it runs from side to side of a vessel, as a square sail does, is set parallel with the line of the keel. In fact, they knew several forms of it,

88 LEFT A sprit-rigged craft depicted in a relief on a tombstone dating from the 2nd or 3rd century AD. Archaeological Museum, Istanbul.

89 ABOVE Detail of a relief depicting a sprit-rigged craft. Behind the sail the sculptor has carefully indicated the sprit that supported it. Sarcophagus in the Ny-Carlsberg Glyptothek, Copenhagen, 3rd century AD.

which they used principally on small craft but also on modest-sized coastal freighters. The best attested form is the sprit rig, in which the sail, loosely fastened by its front edge to a stout mast stepped far up in 88 the bows, is supported by a long spar – the sprit – which extends diagonally across the sail from the lower corner near the mast to the peak, 89 the upper outer corner. The other form that was known was the lateen rig, in which a triangular, or nearly triangular, sail hangs from a very 90 long yard that is hoisted on a relatively short mast. The fore-and-aft rig is less efficient when the wind blows from some point astern but more efficient when it blows from some point ahead. Smaller craft found it useful, since their duties tended to take them on courses that followed the convolutions of a coast or required frequent entries into and exits from harbours, courses in which sooner or later they would have to cope with headwinds.

Every ship, then as now, had aboard a number of anchors. In Europe, from the Middle Ages on, the weight an anchor needs was put into the arms and shank, which were made of iron, while the stock (the horizontal crossbar) was most often of wood. The ancients did it the other way around: they made the arms and shank of wood and put the weight into the stock, which was first of stone and then, from the sixth century BC 91
onward, occasionally of stone but more often of lead. Since both these materials survive underwater, divers have recovered hundreds of stocks of all sizes, from very small ones that must have come from a row-boat's anchor to ponderous examples that surely came from the anchors of seagoing vessels. A wreck excavated off Mahdia on the east coast of Tunisia, which was a fair-sized ship of some 230 tons' burden, was carrying at least five anchors, of which the largest had a stock that was just under 8 feet (2.35 m) long and weighed over 1500 pounds (695 kg). The next largest had a stock even longer, about 8 ft 6 in. (2.46 m), but weighed less, some 1380 pounds (628 kg). Off Malta there was found a behemoth that was 13 ft 9 in. (4.20 m) long and weighed a little over 4000 pounds (1850 kg). This is only 400 pounds less than the 'best bower' – the heaviest anchor carried at the bows – of England's mighty *Sovereign of the Seas*, the 100-gun three-decker, over 200 feet in length, that was launched in 1637.

Most anchors with shank and arms of wood and stock of stone or lead had the stock fixed permanently to the shank; a few may have had a removable stock. The ancients also had anchors all of iron. Many of these have been found, and they very often turn out to have a removable stock. This is a great advantage, for, when not in use, an anchor, once its stock is taken off, can be laid out flat on the deck. A well-preserved specimen of an iron anchor with removable stock that belonged to a 92
luxurious barge built for the Roman emperor Caligula (AD 38–42) was recovered from Lake Nemi south of Rome (see Chapter 10); numerals inscribed on the stock give its weight, 1275 Roman pounds or 917 English pounds (417 kg). In appearance it is astonishingly like a modern anchor, but there is no unbroken line of development linking the ancient anchor with removable stock to the modern – the admiralty anchor as it is called. The ancient version, despite its manifest convenience, passed out of use after the end of ancient times and had to be reinvented. It reappears in the eighteenth century, and in 1852 was introduced into the British navy by a decree of the Admiralty, hence its modern name.

90 A lateen-rigged craft. Relief on a tombstone found near Piraeus and dating from the 2nd century AD. National Archaeological Museum, Athens.

Large merchantmen had windlasses and capstans; these were indispensable for handling their weighty anchors. Anchors were carried at the stern as well as in the bows. When, for example, the vessel that was taking St Paul to Rome, where he was to stand trial, was being inexorably driven by storm in the dark of night into ever shoaling water off the coast of Malta, the crew, in a desperate attempt to halt the ship's way, 'cast four anchors out of the stern, and wished for the day'.[2]

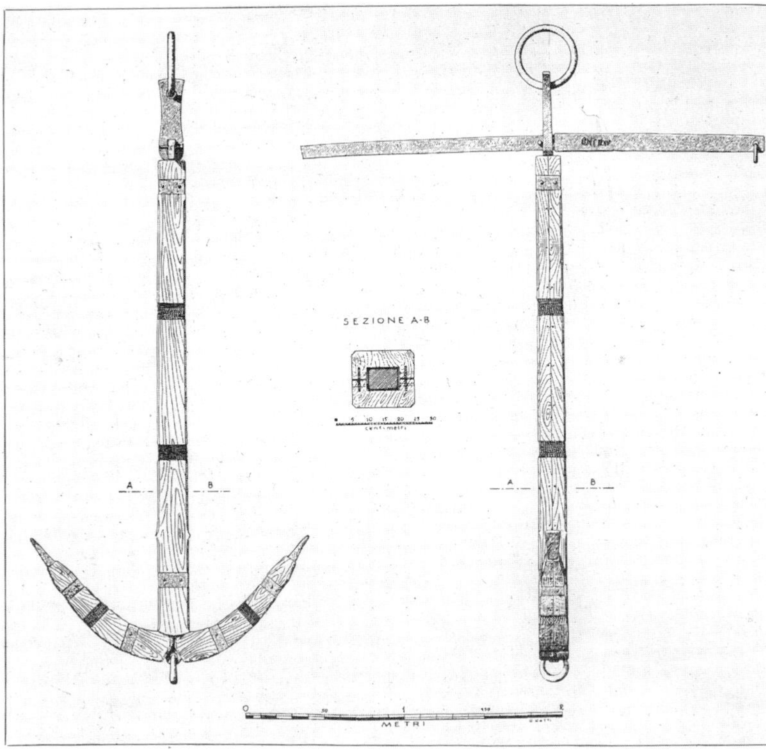

91 ABOVE Large anchor of wood with lead stock, part of the equipment of the imperial houseboats found in Lake Nemi (see Chapter 10). The side of one of the boats, still covered with the lead sheathing that protected its underwater surface, is visible in the background. This photograph was taken before a fire destroyed the boats and most of the objects found with them. First half of the 1st century AD.

92 Iron anchor with removable stock, also part of the equipment of the Nemi boats. The shank and arms were sheathed with wood.

Big merchantmen were plying the Mediterranean at least as early as the fifth century BC. For by this time a standard Greek term for a seagoing freighter was 'ten-thousander', and whether the figure refers to the number of amphoras or of sacks of grain that could be loaded aboard, the capacity works out to some 400 tons. The average British East Indiaman before 1700 was no bigger than this, nor were the first packets that plied between Liverpool and New York a century later. There were, to be sure, multitudes of small carriers tramping along the coast or between islands in ancient times – marine archaeologists, limited to working in relatively shallow water, find more wrecks of these than anything else – but the 'ten-thousanders' or even larger craft took care of the long-distance hauls over open water.

In the Hellenistic Age, the big empires that fostered the phenomenal growth in the size of war galleys did the same for merchantmen. This age saw the launching not only of the greatest war galley recorded in antiquity, Ptolemy IV's mammoth 'forty' (see Chapter 7), but also of the greatest sailing ship. Like the 'forty', it was so memorable a creation that it was written up and hence preserved for history. It was built at the order of Hiero II, king of Syracuse 270–215 BC, to carry grain, the commodity that bulked largest in ancient commerce. Athenaeus, who provides the fullest description of Ptolemy's unique man-of-war, balances it with an even fuller one of Hiero's unique freighter. Hiero, he reports,

> for the materials, collected timber from Mt Etna . . .; then, partly from Italy and partly from Sicily, the wood for treenails and pegs, the upper and lower parts of the frames, and other elements; for cordage, esparto from Spain and hemp and pitch from the Rhone valley; and the rest of his needs from a variety of places. He recruited carpenters and other craftsmen, chose one of them, Archias of Corinth, to be foreman, pressed him to set right to work, and gave the project his personal attention daily. Since there were 300 craftsmen, exclusive of assistants, working on the materials, half of the ship was finished in six months, down to the sheathing of each area, as it was completed, with lead sheets. He gave orders to launch this portion so that the rest of the work could be carried out afloat. After much discussion of how the launching should be done, Archimedes, the engineer, carried it out by himself along with a handful of assistants. He constructed a screw-windlass which drew that huge craft down to the sea. . . . The rest of the ship took another six months.[3]

Hiero was lucky in that he did not have to go far for the wood he needed. The slopes of Mt Etna in his day were still covered with forests of pine and fir which no doubt supplied the timber for the planking. The treenails – the long pegs that held the planks to the frames – and the short pegs that locked the mortises and tenons were probably of oak, and the frames of oak or cypress, both of which grew in southern Italy and Sicily. He was equally lucky in that the greatest engineer of ancient times, Archimedes, was a citizen of Syracuse and hence was at hand to work out a way of drawing the massive hull off the stocks down into the water.

The report continues with the description of the interior – the part that was finished off after the hull had been launched – and dwells on the richness of the fittings. Hiero certainly expected that he and his family and members of his court would be taking voyages in the vessel, for the facilities provided were as sumptuous as those of a modern *de luxe* liner. They included cabins with highly decorated mosaic floors, promenades adorned with potted plants, a gymnasium, a bath complex (it consisted of three copper tubs for hot baths and a fifty-gallon wash-basin of coloured marble), a reading room with library, and a magnificent chapel to Aphrodite, presumably the guardian deity of the ship. Hiero must have thought that his luxurious vessel would be an irresistible target for attack, for he fitted it with every form of naval defence from fighting towers to catapults.

It had three masts. The hunt for a tree tall enough to be made into a mainmast for a ship this size was not easy; finally a suitable candidate 'was located only with great difficulty in the mountains of Bruttium [south-east Italy] by a man from Sybotis; Phileas of Tauromenium [Taranto], the engineer, had it hauled down to the shore.'[4] Since the hauling of the huge tree from the depths of a thick forest to the shore was an even greater accomplishment than finding it, the man responsible earns mention of his name and not just his birthplace.

Archimedes made another important contribution to the ship besides coming up with a way to launch it. Emptying the amount of bilge-water that would collect in its cavernous hull posed a formidable problem. He solved it by installing a water pump of a special type that was his own invention.

Athenaeus closes his description with a list of the cargo taken aboard on the maiden voyage:

> The vessel was loaded with 60,000 measures of grain, 10,000 jars of preserved Sicilian fish, 20,000 talents of wool, and 20,000 talents of miscellaneous cargo; in addition, there were the provisions for the crew. When Hiero heard that, of all the harbours it was to call at, some would not accommodate the ship at all and others were risky, he decided to send it as a gift to King Ptolemy in Alexandria.[5]

At a minimal estimate, the items listed amount to just short of 2000 tons; this biggest of all ancient sailing vessels must have been almost the size of Nelson's *Victory.* The Ptolemy to whom Hiero gave it was probably Ptolemy III, ruler of Egypt from 246 to 221 BC. He was the logical choice: the harbour of Alexandria, formed by two long moles and equipped with a famed lighthouse that was one of the seven wonders of the ancient world, was among the very few that could accommodate this mighty ship, and the land of Egypt was among the very few that exported sufficient quantities of grain to exploit its capacity.

Egypt's grain, in fact, was ultimately responsible for bringing into being the largest fleet of big carriers in ancient history – or, for that matter, much of later history. After Augustus conquered the country and made it part of the Roman Empire, it supplied one-third of the grain needed to feed the population of Rome, some 135,000 tons annually. To get this much grain every year from Alexandria to Rome called for highly developed organisation. Except for emergencies, the ancients limited their sailing to the season when the weather was most dependable, roughly from the beginning of April to October. The winds over the waters between Rome and Alexandria during this period blow prevailingly from the west. This meant that the voyage from Rome, made with a favourable wind all the way, was quick and easy, taking normally no more than two to three weeks. But it also meant that the return to Rome, made against foul winds all the way, was slow and arduous; a month was very good time, usually it took two, and not uncommonly almost three. As a result, ships that started from Alexandria could squeeze in no more than two round-trips a season, and that only if they were lucky enough to have a quick turn-around at either end; probably most managed but one. Ships starting from Rome could squeeze in at best one round-trip plus a return to Alexandria, where they would spend the winter and be ready to load up and shove off with the opening of the sailing season in the spring.

The solution to hauling the large amount of cargo involved in so limited a time was the use of oversize freighters. We know how big they could be, thanks to a lucky accident. Sometime around the middle of the second century AD, one of them met a spell of bad weather, was driven far off course, and landed up in Piraeus, the port of Athens. Athens by this time had long since ceased to be an important centre and was little more than a sleepy university town. The news that one of the famous Alexandria–Rome grain carriers could be seen in the harbour drew everybody down to the waterfront, including Lucian, the essayist we mentioned earlier in this chapter. He recorded his impressions of it:

> What a size the ship was! One hundred and eighty feet in length, the ship's carpenter told me, the beam more than a quarter of that, and forty-four feet from the deck to the bottom, the deepest point in the bilge. What a mast it had, what a yard it carried, what a forestay held it up! The way the sternpost rose in a gradual curve with a gilded goose-head set on the tip of it, matched at the opposite end by the forward, more flattened, rise of the prow with the figure of Isis, the goddess the ship was named after, on each side! And the rest of the decoration, the paintings, the red pennant on the main yard, the anchors and capstans and winches on the foredeck, the accommodations toward the stern – it all seemed like marvels to me! The crew must have been as big as an army. They told me she carried so much grain that it would be enough to feed every mouth in Athens for a year.[6]

It was indeed a mighty vessel, able to carry, to judge from its dimensions, between 1200 and 1300 tons; the anchor stock weighing over 4000 pounds that was found off Malta may well have come from a similar ship. It compares with the biggest of the British East Indiamen, those that came into use at the beginning of the nineteeth century. If all its sisters on the run were as capacious, a fleet of about eighty would have been sufficient to ferry the 135,000 tons of grain that Egypt sent every year to Rome.

The sailing ships of the ancient world performed another key service besides hauling cargo: they transported passengers. And there were a good many to take care of since going by sea, particularly if a long distance was involved, was most often quicker and always more comfortable than going by land.

The passenger ship did not exist in antiquity. Travellers did as they were to do for many centuries thereafter: they went down to the waterfront and asked around until they found a merchantman scheduled to sail to their destination or at least to some port along their line of course. 'In Constantinople', writes Libanius, a Greek literary figure of the fourth century AD, 'I went down to the Great Harbour and made the rounds asking about vessels sailing for Athens.'[7] For those departing from Italy for the Near East or vice versa, the first choice was one of the Rome–Alexandria grain freighters, since the big ships offered not only room and safety but the quickest possible crossings. When, for example, the Jewish princeling Agrippa was planning to leave Rome for Palestine in AD 37, the emperor Caligula advised him not to take the land route that followed the coasts around to Palestine,

> which was long and tiring but, waiting for the summer winds, to take a direct sailing to Alexandria. The ships are crack sailing craft and their skippers the most experienced there are; they drive the vessels like racehorses on an unswerving course that goes straight as a die.[8]

Once at Alexandria, Agrippa could easily cover the short segment to Palestine either by land or sea. St Paul started the journey that ended in shipwreck off Malta at Caesarea in Palestine. The Roman centurion in charge of the group of prisoners that included him put them aboard a vessel headed for the coast of Asia Minor; it happened to be in the harbour ready to leave, and Asia Minor was on the line of its course to Rome. When it arrived there at the port of Myra, by great good luck 'the centurion found a ship of Alexandria sailing into Italy; and he put us therein'.[9] It was one of the big freighters of the grain fleet, which had stopped at Myra on its way to Rome.

Since the carrying of passengers was only incidental to the carrying of cargo, ancient merchantmen provided the minimum in facilities. There were no cabins, apart from a few in the deckhouse that was a regular feature of seagoing ships, and these were reserved for the skipper or important personages, such as the owner of the cargo or his agent. They 84
served no food. About all they furnished was water and deck space. Travellers came aboard with their servant or servants – anyone on the move had at least one; only exiles, refugees, vagabonds or the like travelled

without any – loaded down with bedding, food and wine. When it was time to eat, the servants would prepare a meal for their masters, taking turns at the ship's galley to cook it, and when it was time to go to sleep they would set up little tent-like shelters on deck for them to sleep under; during the Mediterranean summer, when most sailing took place, this very likely was preferable to being quartered in a cabin.

When a ship ran into danger, the passengers' only hope of survival was to cling to it, for there were no lifeboats; ubiquitous today, these were unknown in ancient times. Ships had merely a single small boat to serve as jolly boat, which normally was not kept on deck but towed astern. 83–4
When the vessel carrying Paul from Myra to Rome faced almost certain shipwreck off Malta, the crew tried to sneak off in the ship's boat and save their own skins. Paul caught them in the act and got the officer and soldiers who were accompanying him to stop them by stating the bald truth: 'Except these abide in the ship, ye cannot be saved';[10] in other words, without the seamen aboard to handle it, the ship was doomed and with it the only chance of salvation for every soul aboard.

Travellers who were anxious to avoid such perils, inherent in crossings over open water, had an alternative: merchant galleys, which normally stayed close to shore. Merchant galleys, made for transporting passengers

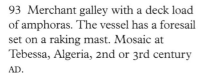

93 Merchant galley with a deck load of amphoras. The vessel has a foresail set on a raking mast. Mosaic at Tebessa, Algeria, 2nd or 3rd century AD.

and cargo and not for carrying marines or launching ram attacks, go as far back in maritime history as the war galley (see Chapter 5). They were ugly ducklings compared with their sleek military relatives, being broader in beam and heavier in build. Moreover, they never had more than one level of rowers, since the oars were merely auxiliary; they depended on 93
wind as much as possible and turned to manpower only when strictly necessary, when becalmed or when doubling a headland against a foul breeze or entering or leaving harbour. They customarily tramped along coasts, picking up or dropping off people and goods at the ports on the way. But there were some that saw use on open water, chiefly for crossings during which delay could be damaging. Rome, for example, needed a steady supply of wild animals for its gladiatorial games. These were mostly hunted in Africa, and to get them from the ports on its north shore across the Mediterranean to Italy they were often loaded aboard merchant galleys. The handlers wanted to hold to a minimum the time the creatures had to spend in cramped cages on a pitching and rolling vessel, and the galleys, able to keep going wind or no wind, were a better bet than sailing ships.

The history of ancient merchantmen reveals both accomplishments and limitations. The shipwrights of antiquity built vessels as strong as those of later ages and bigger than those of most; the aggregation of oversize freighters that carried grain from Alexandria to Rome, for example, was not to be matched until the eighteenth century. But because of their method of construction, in which the strength was placed mainly in a shell of edge-joined planks, they were limited in the shapes they could give to their hulls; later ages, with far more flexibility, were able to turn out hulls of better design and greater variety. In rig the ancients never advanced very far. Throughout they depended for drive chiefly on a single great mainsail, a rig that was safe but slow. The Middle Ages saw no improvement. It was not until the fifteenth century that seamen took the vital step of superimposing sails and thereby launched the development that culminated in the towering tiers of canvas of the nineteenth-century clippers.

94 A small cargo vessel, moored in the shallows before a beach or a river bank, is being unloaded. The mast has been unstepped and rests horizontally in mast crutches. The triangular cleats along it are to enable deckhands to climb up it. Since it was retractable it could not easily be fitted with a rope ladder for getting aloft, as on seagoing craft (see Figs 85, 93), and its stays were presumably too light for men to haul themselves up on, hence the need for climbing cleats. Aft of the heel of the mast is the cylinder of a capstan; the horizontal levers for heaving it round have been stowed away, leaving visible the circular sockets into which they fitted. The presence and location of the capstan indicates that, in addition to travelling under its own power, the vessel was designed for being towed upstream; the towing line would be brought to the mast and, passing over a block on it, be made fast to the capstan aft (see Fig. 96). Relief in the cathedral of Salerno, 3rd century AD.

10

Along the Coasts, in Harbours, on Rivers

By far the greatest number of ships plying the ancient Mediterranean were the small freighters that tramped along the coasts, the sort that the marine archaeologists, necessarily confined to working near shore, have found off Yassi Ada, Kyrenia, and many other places. They were built in the same way as the big merchantmen that sailed the open water, of planks joined edge to edge with mortises and tenons, and they had the same basic variation in the shape of the prow, sometimes rounded, sometimes extended at the waterline into a projecting forefoot. The key difference was in rig. They, too, were mostly square-rigged, but generally with only a mainsail, often set on a retractable mast. And some were fore-and-aft rigged. 94

What these coastal craft inevitably lacked was the deck space that their big sisters could supply. The great ship that foundered at Malta with St Paul aboard (see Chapter 9) was carrying 276 passengers, and presumably there was room on the deck for all of them, either singly or in groups, to stake out a spot on which to set up a shelter for sleeping. In the *Satyricon*, the picaresque novel by the Roman satirist Petronius, the protagonists travel on a ship whose deck was ample enough to accommodate a bloody brawl in which everyone aboard, passengers as well as crew, mixed in and to enable the opposing sides to draw safely apart when they had had their fill of flailing at each other. But the likes of, say, the Yassi Ada vessel, with an overall length of but 70 feet (21 m), had no such profusion of space to offer. And the Kyrenia vessel, 45 feet (13.7 m) overall, had merely some scant decking at prow and stern.

We get a glimpse of what it was like to travel on these little craft from

a letter that has survived written by Synesius, an aristocratic Greek intellectual who converted to Christianity and eventually became a bishop; in AD 404 he booked passage on a small freighter to go from Alexandria to his home town of Cyrene some 500 nautical miles westward along the coast – about a five-day voyage under normal circumstances – and on arrival sent a lively, chatty account of the voyage to his brother back in Alexandria. We must take some of what he says with a grain of salt; Synesius was as concerned with entertaining the reader as with informing him.

The ship was owner-operated, and the owner, Amarantus by name, was, according to Synesius, 'crushed to death by a load of debt'.[1] This is one of the aspects calling for that grain of salt: no doubt Amarantus owed money, since shipowners, then as now, commonly worked on credit, but Synesius' repeated snide allusions make it quite clear that he exaggerates for comic effect. There was a crew of twelve, all, Synesius claims,

> ordinary farm boys who up to last year had never touched an oar. The one thing they all shared in common was having some bodily defect. And, so long as we were in no danger, they made jokes about this and called each other by their misfortunes instead of their real names – Cripple, Ruptured, One-Arm, Squint; each and every one had his nickname. All this rather amused us. But, in time of need, it was no laughing matter; we had reason to groan over these very defects, since there were more than fifty passengers, about one-third of them women and mostly young and pretty. Don't be envious: a curtain walled us off, a good strong one, a veritable wall of Semiramis [legendary builder of Babylon with its massive walls] in the eyes of decent temperate men. . . .[2]

As soon as Amarantus cleared the harbour of Alexandria, continues Synesius,

> he decided to make straight for Taposiris [a town on the coast about twenty-five miles west of Alexandria] with all sail flying and take a try at Scylla, the one in the story books we get so scared at. When we realised this and, a hair's breadth from disaster, let out a shout, we just managed to force him to give up doing battle with the rocks. Then, spinning the vessel about as if having a change of mind, off he went for the open water, for a while struggling against the sea as best he could but later helped along by a good breeze from the south.[3]

Had Synesius known anything about sailing, he would have been aware of what was happening: Amarantus had started on a long tack landward and extended it just as far as he could, as a good skipper will. He then 'spun the vessel about' – not because of any sudden change of mind, but simply to go on the opposite tack, where, as even the fearful and suspicious Synesius became aware, he was helped by the offshore wind.

Toward evening, the wind started to make up and by midnight a full-fledged storm was raging:

Colour Plate VIII *Olympias*, a modern replica of a trireme, proceeding under oars.

Colour Plate IX The interior of *Olympias*, showing the three levels of rowers.

Colour Plate X A square-rigged fishing boat. The artist has rendered the lower part of the hull in black, probably to indicate that this area was covered with lead sheathing. Mosaic in the Bardo Museum, Tunis, 3rd century AD.

The men groaned, the women shrieked, everybody called upon God, cried aloud, remembered their dear ones. Only Amarantus was in good spirits, thinking he was going to get out of paying his creditors. . . . I noticed that the soldiers [a large group of the passengers were members of an Arab cavalry unit] had all drawn their swords. I asked why and learned that they preferred to belch up their souls to the open air, on deck, rather than gurgle them up to the sea. True descendants of Homer, I thought, and approved of the idea. Then someone called out that all who had any gold should hang it around their neck. Those who had, did so, both gold and anything else of the value of gold. The women not only put on their jewellery but handed out pieces of string to any who needed them. This is a time-honoured practice, and the reason for it is this: you must provide the corpse of someone lost at sea with the money to pay for a funeral so that whoever recovers it, profiting by it, won't mind giving it a little attention. . . .

The ship was rushing along under full canvas because we couldn't shorten sail. Time and again we laid hands on the lines but gave up because they were jammed in the blocks. And secretly we began to be equally afraid that, even if we escaped from the raging sea, we would be approaching land in the dead of night in this helpless condition. Day broke before this happened, and we saw the sun – and never with greater pleasure. As the heat of day came on, the wind moderated, and with the wetness out of the ropes, we were able to use them and handle sail. To replace with a stormsail was impossible – it was in the pawn shop. We took the sail in like the folds of a tunic, and within four hours, we, who had been expecting death, found ourselves disembarking in a remote deserted spot with not a town nor farm nearby for fifteen miles around. The ship was tossing in the open roads (for the spot was no harbour) held by only one anchor – the second anchor had been sold, and Mr Amarantus did not own a third. When we touched beloved land, we embraced it like a living mother.[4]

Synesius no doubt had cause for some of his grumbling. It could not have been very comfortable with over half a hundred people, captain and crew and passengers, all cheek by jowl and all getting mercilessly thrown from one side to the other every time the ship changed tack. And, when the storm came, to the physical discomfort was added the acute mental discomposure caused by the various lugubrious preparations for death, which in the tight quarters no one could escape seeing and hearing. During the emergency caused by the storm every man aboard was called on to lend a hand; we can picture the elegant and fastidious Synesius lined up with the burly Arab cavalrymen and with Squint and Ruptured and the others of the crew as they hauled with might and main on those ropes that stubbornly refused to budge. His words reveal that they were struggling not to brail up the sail but to strip it off and replace it. The ship must have been a lateener, for this is what is done with such a rig: since there is no way to shorten the canvas, the practice is to take off the working sail and substitute a smaller. The lateen-rigged galleys of Venice's great fleets of the fourteenth and fifteenth centuries, for example, carried a series of sails of diminishing sizes to be used for winds of increasing strength.

Harbour Craft

In the ancient world, as today, major ports required the services of two special types of harbour craft, tugs and lighters. Such ports had to accommodate big merchantmen, and big merchantmen furled their sails upon entering, for they could not travel inside harbours under their own power. There was rarely room in which to manoeuvre, and even if there were, the wind could well be contrary or non-existent. Like modern passenger liners or oversize tankers and similar craft, they had to call upon tugboats to move them about. A relief found near Rome's port shows what the ancient version of a tug looked like. It was a stout skiff propelled by several sets of oars and steered not by the customary pair of steering oars, one on each quarter, but by a single oversized oar mounted on the stern; this provided the leverage needed for guiding an unwieldy tow. In the bows was stepped a mast that most likely carried a spritsail; the rig enabled the tug to get to the mouth of the harbour with a wind from almost any quarter and thereby spare the rowers' muscle for the hard pull back. Its skipper would nose up to the arriving vessel's prow and run a line from there to his stern, the rowers would pull till the line was taut, and then, straining at the oars, would haul the vessel to its

84–5

95

95 This heavy dory is a harbour tugboat; the line extending outward and upward from the stern ended at the prow of the vessel it was pulling. Far up in the bows is a mast which was almost certainly rigged with a spritsail (see Fig. 88 and the central ship in Fig. 99), which it would use to get out to where it could pick up its tow. Instead of the usual pair of steering oars, one on each quarter, it has a single oversized oar mounted on the stern, an arrangement no doubt adopted to give greater leverage for guiding an unwieldy tow. Relief on a tomb in the Isola Sacra between Ostia and Portus, 3rd century AD.

assigned place either alongside a dock or, if there was no room there, to an anchorage somewhere in the harbour.

Ships that found a berth at a dock were lucky: they tied up prow first, as was the practice, and all they had to do was throw over a gangplank, 76, 84
and a line of hardworking stevedores carried the amphoras or sacks or whatever down to the dock. Ships that put up at an anchorage had need of the second special type of harbour craft, the lighters. These were open broad flat-bottomed craft that were propelled by long sweeps or, where the water was shallow enough, were poled. Cargo from the vessels at anchor was lowered into them and they ferried it to the shore.

And in major harbours, alongside the heavy and plain barges and tugs, there were to be seen flitting about the elegant and gaily coloured pleasure XI
yachts of the wealthy.

Rivercraft

Major ports are often to be found at the mouths of rivers. Among ancient examples are Ostia, the original port of Rome, and Portus, the man-made harbour that succeeded it, at the mouth of the Tiber; Marseilles near the mouth of the Rhone, Antioch on the Orontes and numerous others. Such a location enabled goods arriving at the port to continue inland by water, always the cheapest and most efficient form of transportation in ancient times. Alexandria, for example, owed much of its importance to its position at the mouth of the Nile, a river that made an ideal waterway; as mentioned earlier (Chapter 2), it is blessed with a prevailing wind that, blowing opposite to the direction of the flow, permits boats on it to sail upstream as well as down. Most rivers are not so accommodating, and, until the introduction of steam power, the only way to buck their currents was by towing. Special craft were designed for this, of shallow draft and with a mast stepped forward of amidships; occasionally they carried a capstan on the poop. Teams, usually of men 94, 96
but at times of oxen, would trudge along a path that followed the bank, clutching the end of a long line that either ran to the top of the mast or 97
passed over a block there and continued to the stern. The running of the towline to a mast elevated it, thereby keeping it from catching on brush, unevennesses in the ground, and similar obstacles. The capstan was for those spots along a river where the current ran too swiftly for the teams to make progress. They would tie their end of the line around a tree or rocky projection; the crew would then put the other end on the capstan, and, heaving it round, would winch the vessel ahead.

At Ostia and Portus at the mouth of the Tiber, practically all the cargo that arrived was destined for Rome some thirteen miles upstream. To facilitate moving it there a special type of local vessel, the *caudicaria*, was developed, one that could be sailed or towed. Its hull was like that of any small freighter, and its rig consisted of a spritsail on a mast stepped well

97 A small rivercraft being hauled by a towline made fast to the top of the towing mast. On larger rivercraft the line would pass over a block on the mast and be made fast to a capstan near the stern. Relief found at Cabrières-d'Aigues and now in the Musée Calvet, Avignon; 3rd century AD.

96 The scene is presumably the harbour of Portus, just north of the mouth of the Tiber and connected to it by a canal. A cargo of amphoras is being transferred from a seagoing vessel (right) to a rivercraft (left) that will carry it through the canal and up the Tiber to Rome. As on the rivercraft pictured in Fig. 94, the mast is fitted with climbing cleats and there is a capstan on the stern to receive the towline when the vessel was being hauled upstream. Mosaic in the Foro delle Corporazioni, Ostia. About AD 200.

forward in the bows. Thus it was able to raise sail and under its own power go about the harbour or along the nearby coasts picking up cargo; when it had a load it headed into the river, dropped its canvas, rigged a towline to the mast, and got pulled to Rome.

A number of representations have survived in which the *caudicaria* appears, including one that portrays the craft taking part in a crisis at
sea. It is a relief carved on the front face of a sarcophagus; presumably 99
it pictures how the deceased met his end. The scene is the mouth of the harbour at Portus on a windy day when the waves were running high. A boy – or perhaps a man – has fallen out of a tiny skiff in which he had been rowing. Two vessels race to the rescue, a *caudicaria* in the lead and a square-rigged freighter behind it. At that very moment another freighter, also square-rigged, approaches from the opposite direction. The skipper of the *caudicaria*, suddenly aware that he is in danger of a head-on collision, has given up all thought of making the rescue. The ship behind has taken over that task, and one of the crew is leaning anxiously over the bow, ready to reach a hand out to the boy in the water. He is not aware of help from this quarter; his gaze is riveted despairingly on the ship nearest him which, confronted by its own peril, can no longer bother with him.

The *caudicaria* was developed for use on the Tiber. Other streams,
too, had distinctive types of rivercraft. Boatmen on the Rhine or Moselle, 98
for example, used vessels that were steered by a single steering oar
mounted on the stern. Boatmen of the Saar used sails made of leather 100
stiffened by horizontal battens that reached from one side to the other. Boatmen on the Danube used stout tubby craft; in AD 113 the Roman emperor Trajan erected at Rome a great column ornamented with a series of reliefs depicting events in his conquest of what is today Romania,

98 RIGHT Rivercraft of the Rhine or Moselle. The short mast set forward of amidships is a towing mast. The vessel is steered, not by the usual pair of steering oars on the quarters, but by a single oar mounted on the stern. Relief on a tombstone in the Mittelrheinisches Landesmuseum, Mainz. Mid-1st century AD.

99 The mouth of the harbour at Portus. The structure at the far left presumably stood on the end of the arm that embraced one side of the harbour basin; at the far right is the lighthouse marking the harbour entrance. A boy or man is in the water, having fallen out of his skiff. The ship in the centre, it would seem, was racing to the rescue but was distracted when it found itself on a collision course with a vessel entering the harbour. The ship to the left has taken over the rescue attempt. The ships to right and left are ordinary square-rigged merchantmen; the one in the centre is a sprit-rigged *caudicaria*, the special type of rivercraft favoured for use on the Tiber. Relief on a sarcophagus probably from Ostia and now in the Ny-Carlsberg Glyptothek, Copenhagen; 3rd century AD

and these include representations of the local Danube river boats transporting his army's supplies.

In Egypt the Nile not only enjoyed ideal wind conditions but was navigable without a break for some 700 miles, from Alexandria on the coast of the Mediterranean to the First Cataract, thus offering water transport the length of the land. Inevitably it fostered the development of a rich variety of rivercraft; all sizes and shapes were to be seen on it, from humble canoes made of bundles of papyrus reeds to lordly *thala-* XII
megoi ('cabin-carriers'), the costly yachts for transporting government 101
officials, nobility and similar VIPs. Ptolemy IV, who ordered the building of the grandiose 'forty' for his navy (see Chapter 7), matched it with an 67–8
equally grandiose *thalamegos* for his own use, a veritable floating palace. Athenaeus, the Greek writer to whom we owe the description of the 'forty', furnishes one of this remarkable craft as well. It was 300 feet (91 102
m) overall (in other words, longer by over a third than Nelson's *Victory*), and 45 feet (13.7 m) in beam, rose to a height of 40 feet (12 m), but, designed for use on a river, drew very little water. Like the 'forty', it was a catamaran: upon a pair of shallow hulls was set a lofty superstructure that housed accommodations more sumptuous than those of the most sumptuous yachts afloat today. There were two decks. Each was circled by a promenade; the one on the lower deck was completely closed in,

100 RIGHT Rivercraft of the Sarre or Moselle. The battens running horizontally the full width of the sail are unusual; they probably indicate that the sail was of leather. Relief in the Rheinisches Landesmuseum, Trier, 2nd–3rd century AD.

101 ABOVE A graceful yacht, fitted with an ample cabin, sails down the Nile. Detail from a mosaic in the Palazzo Barberini, Palestrina, Italy. Early 1st century BC. (See also Colour Plate XII, opposite p. 144.)

102 Reconstruction of the grandiose houseboat of Ptolemy IV (ruled 222–205 BC).

offering strollers total relief from Egypt's burning sun, while that on the upper, lined with windows, was for the evening or the cooler hours of the day. There were no less than four dining rooms. The main one was on the upper deck; its pride was a magnificent coffered ceiling with sculptured ornamentation that gleamed with gilding. The second dining hall, on the lower deck, was notable for a peristyle of columns of marble imported from India. The third was in the women's quarters – the living arrangements on Ptolemy's *thalamegos*, like those in every Greek house, shut the women off in an area of their own – and was just as richly decorated as the main one. Lastly, on the roof of the superstructure was a fourth for dining *al fresco*; it was open to the sky, although discreetly shielded from view by purple curtains on all sides. There must have been sizeable dining facilities for the army of servants aboard, but Athenaeus does not deign to mention such a mundane feature. The staterooms were equally magnificent, but they all accommodated a number of occupants; the modern taste for privacy was unknown to the ancients. The master stateroom, for example, panelled in choice woods and boasting columns whose capitals were sheathed in ivory and gold, had no less than twenty beds; it was, in effect, a dormitory. Religion was provided for by two chapels, one to Aphrodite and the other to Dionysus; the latter included a niche, encrusted with precious stones, where statues of the royal family were displayed.

It all sounds incredible. But Athenaeus can be trusted, for there is no question that such mighty vessels floated on inland waters in ancient times. The incontrovertible proof is provided by the vessels built for the Roman emperor Caligula that we had occasion to mention earlier (Chapter 3).

In the Alban Hills some twenty miles south-east of Rome lies Lake Nemi, a picturesque body of water surrounded by precipitous cliffs. It is small, only three and a half miles in circumference, but deep, over 100 feet (30.5 m). The lovely wooded area around it was in ancient times the awesomely sacred grove of the goddess Diana, whence the lake's name: *nemus* means 'grove' in Latin. As early as the Middle Ages it was rumoured that there were ships lying on its bottom, ships that had been built by a Roman emperor. The rumour was nourished by objects that fishermen kept bringing up in their nets, of a kind that could come from such ships. About the middle of the fifteenth century the noble whose estates included the land around the lake decided to attempt to raise them. He assigned the task to no less a personage than Leon Battista Alberti, the renowned Renaissance scholar, architect and engineer. With the primitive means at his disposal, all Alberti succeeded in doing was to bring up a chunk of timber, but it served to substantiate the rumour. A century later a renewed attempt yielded still more timbers. Three centuries passed before, in 1827, yet another try was made, and this produced something new: pieces of coloured marble and mosaic. Then, in 1895,

103 LEFT This splendid bronze relief of a Medusa head was fished up from Lake Nemi; it was a decorative fitting from one of the great houseboats of Caligula that had sunk there. First half of the 1st century AD.

104 RIGHT The remains of one of Caligula's houseboats, laid bare by the pumping out of the waters of Lake Nemi in 1928–32.

105 The boat seen from the prow.

an ambitious effort, profiting from the more sophisticated equipment by then available, achieved startling results: the finds included not only more coloured marble and mosaic tesserae, but some finely decorated bronze
103 fittings. Moreover, it was ascertained that there were two vessels, one nearer shore and one farther out, both huge and both fitted out in costly fashion.

The attempts hitherto had all been carried out by individuals either for their own gratification or, in some cases, their own profit from the sale of what they had found. In 1927 the Italian government stepped in; the ships after all were not only part of the country's archaeological heritage but a unique part, totally unlike any other of its remains from the past, rich and varied as these were. A commission whose membership included hydraulic engineers was charged with finding a way of saving the priceless relics. They came up with a plan to empty the lake of its water. It was a formidable, a monumental project, but they carried it off. Pumping started in 1928, and by 3 September the following year the vessel nearer shore, which had been about 16 to 40 feet (5–12 m) below the surface, was high and dry. On 30 January 1930, the second, at the
104 much greater depth of about 49 to 65 feet (15–20 m), began to emerge. By 1932, despite some heartbreaking setbacks, the project was complete: both ships had been removed from the floor of the lake and put in a hastily constructed shed. By 1936 they were enthroned in a splendid museum on the shore, built specially to house them.

Their stay there was short: they became casualties of the Second World War. On 28 May 1944 a German artillery battery suddenly took up a position in front of the museum, and the Italian custodians, who had remained on duty till then, were brusquely told to leave. In the ensuing

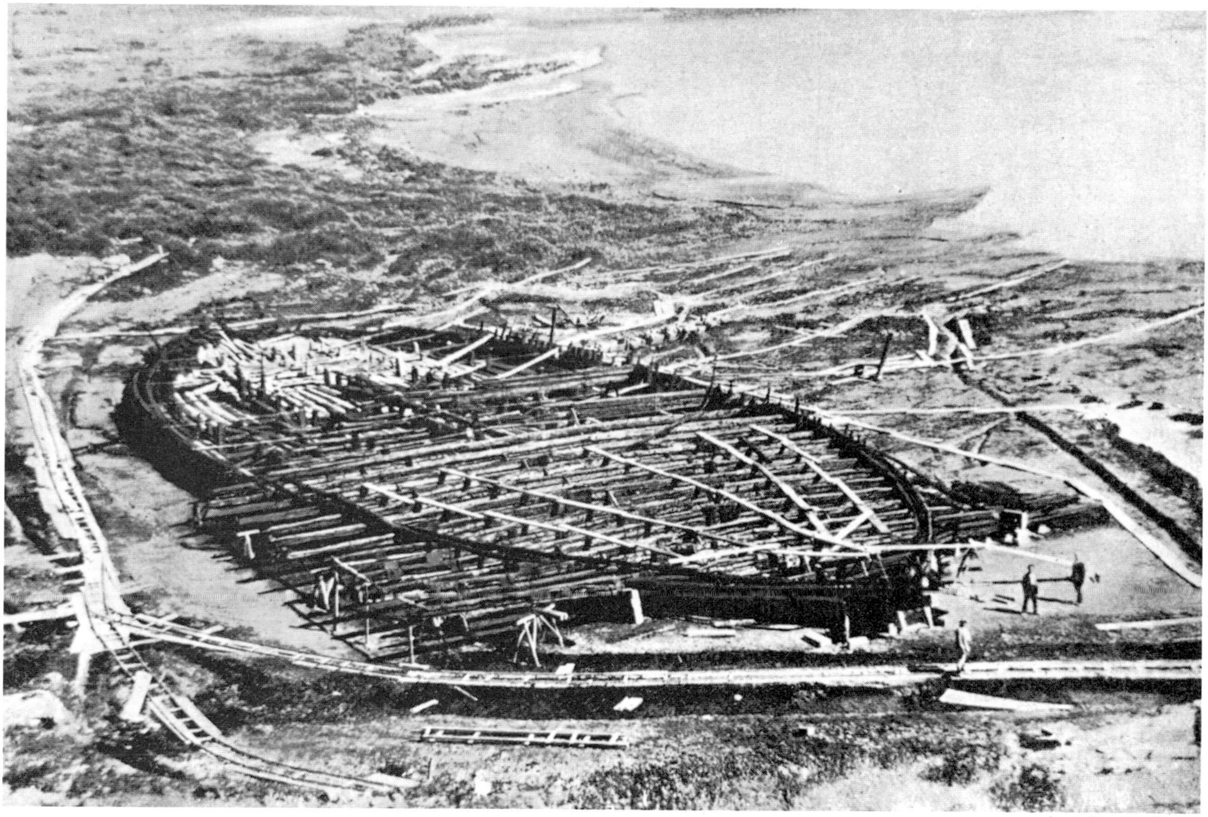

days, despite bombing and shelling of the position that resulted in several hits on the museum, the boats remained unharmed. On the night of the 31st, a fire was observed inside the museum; it gradually spread until flames filled the whole building. On the night of 2 June, the German unit moved out, and early that morning the Italian custodians entered the ravaged building. They found the ships reduced to charred timbers and ashes. A committee of investigation concluded that the soldiers of the battery, before making their retreat, had deliberately set them on fire.

The vessels had been lost – but not what they had to contribute to nautical history, for they had been exhaustively measured and photographed and replicated in exact models. What was most striking was their immense size. Though well short of the 300–foot length of Ptolemy's *thalamegos*, they far surpassed its beam of 45 feet. The one nearer shore, 234 feet long, had a beam of 65 feet (71.3 × 20 m). The other was only 213 feet long but it was all of 77 feet in beam (65 × 23.6 m). The shaft of one of the steering oars was recovered; it was a mighty pole 17 inches (43 cm) in diameter and almost 38 feet (11.5 m) long. The construction of the hull was a model of the ancient shipwright's art: the planks were joined by mortise and tenon joints set 4 inches (10 cm) apart; the framing was powerful, with the frames set 20 inches (50 cm) apart; and the whole exterior surface was covered with lead sheathing laid over a fabric liner 105
impregnated with pitch. Although both hulls came to a point at prow and stern, they were in effect vast flat-bottomed barges, obviously designed to carry imposing superstructures – superstructures that, unfortunately, did not survive. But remains of their decor and fittings were recovered, and to judge from these they housed quarters as palatial as on Ptolemy's *thalamegos*. Floors had been covered with pavements of coloured mosaic or of pieces of coloured marble set in intricate patterns. Walls had been veneered with coloured marble. The tips of beams and of stanchions, the heads of the steering oars, and other such elements had been capped with bronze fittings adorned with sculptures of the highest quality. There 103
were railings of bronze, whose uprights were finished off with sculptures.

Pieces of lead tubing were found in the hulls with the name of the emperor Caligula (AD 38–42) stamped on them, revealing that it was he who was responsible for the building of the vessels. Caligula was notorious for his lavish outlays on grandiose projects and showy displays. He was equally notorious for his orgiastic parties, and earlier commentators were certain that this is what the Nemi ships were for, conjuring up visions of vinous and sexual goings-on amid their splendours. Later commentators were more sober. They kept in mind the unusual location, at anchor in a sheltered lake in the midst of a most hallowed sanctuary, a location that called for solemn religious rites rather than wild revelries. The ships, they concluded, must have housed richly adorned chapels for worship, chambers for meditation and similar accommodations, not garish banqueting halls and ballrooms. They are surely right.

11

In the North

In early September 1937 Edward Wright, then in his teens, was walking, as he had done for years, with his brother along the north bank of the Humber river on the look-out for ancient remains. At Ferriby, about eight miles west of Hull, one of them spotted something unusual, the ends of three pieces of wood protruding from the clayey mud of the bank. It was a momentous discovery; the Wrights were to spend every spare moment they had for the rest of their lives unearthing and studying it. The pieces turned out to be part of a boat built of massive planks of oak – a big boat, some 52 ft 6 in. (16 m) in length 106
and slightly over 9 ft 10 in. (3 m) at its widest point. Excavation produced the remains of several others as well, but the first find proved to be the best preserved.

The planks had been set edge to edge and sewn together with withies of yew; on the inside, battens had been laid over the seams and the stitches ran over these, holding them in place – a system not unlike that found on the Cheops boat (Chapter 2) and still used in parts of the world 14
today. The hull was rounded in shape and hence each plank met its neighbours at an angle; to get a snug fit, the edge of one was rounded into a tongue and the edge of the matching plank hollowed into a groove to receive it. Caulking was still required to make the seams watertight, and this was done with moss. The boat had been propelled by paddles, as the remains of several revealed; there was room for up to nine paddlers a side. There may even have been a sail for downwind travel.

The sophistication and skill of the carpentry, carried out in so tough a wood as oak, convinced those who studied it that it was beyond the technical capability of primitive times; that the boat must date from the post-Roman centuries, even, according to some, the early Middle Ages. Decades later, when carbon-14 dating became available, tests were run and the results were astonishing: the wood dated from around 1400 BC. The boat was thus a product of Britain's Bronze Age, and by far the oldest example of a planked boat from northern Europe. Early evidence for small primitive craft, such as skin boats or dugout canoes, had been found in many parts of northern Europe. But the remains at Ferriby proved that, as far back as the mid-second millennium BC, sizeable vessels built by skilled shipwrights were sailing the waters of its rivers and bays.

The Wrights' discovery was a great stroke of luck. The next example from northern Europe of a boat built of planks dates some 1200 years later, from the second century BC. Yet it is clearly a relative of the Ferriby boats, long and narrow and of massive planks sewn together. Then, in the first century AD, a new type of construction makes an appearance, a type that must have been widespread, for examples have turned up in England, Belgium, Holland and Switzerland. The planks, still massive, are no longer sewn together but nailed to frames. The best evidence comes from Zwammerdam, on the mouth of the Rhine near Rotterdam. 107
Here was unearthed a group of boats that were almost rectangular in

106 The best preserved of the Ferriby boats after removal to the National Maritime Museum, Greenwich. About 1400 BC.

shape, with flat bottoms and straight sides. The shipwright had started by laying the planks of the bottom lengthwise side by side. Next he placed floor timbers across them, and then, from the underside, drove long nails through both planks and floor timbers and clenched the ends. The planks forming the sides he nailed to side frames. One of the Zwammerdam boats shows that he had selected for the floor timbers pieces of wood 108
that at one end had branches growing out more or less upright and hence able to serve as a side frame for one side; by alternating these, one with the upright branch to starboard and the next with the upright branch to port, he ended up with side frames for both sides. The side planks were not set edge to edge, as were the bottom planks, but with the upper overlapping the lower – an anticipation of the technique that was brought to perfection in the Viking ships. All the seams were caulked with moss.

The makers of these vessels certainly knew the Mediterranean way of assembling a ship by setting all the planks edge to edge and securing the 24–6
edges to each other by means of multitudinous mortise and tenon joints (Chapters 3, 9). The Romans, after all, ruled much of north-western Europe for centuries, and so it is no surprise that the remains of boats

107 The Zwammerdam boat, dating from the 1st century AD.

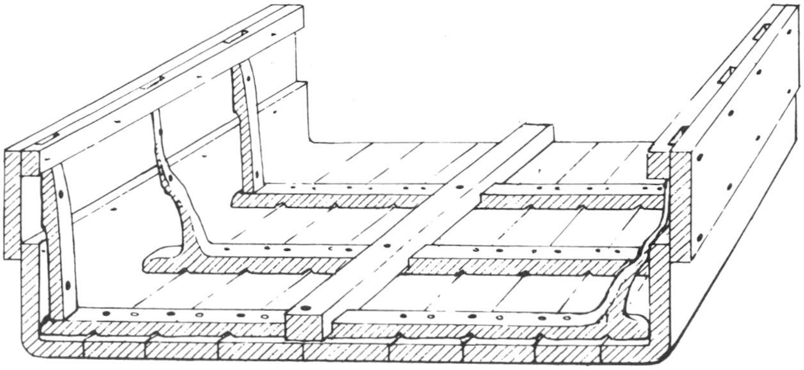

108 Cross-section of the Zwammerdam boat. The side frame on the right of the foremost frame is formed by a natural growth from the wood selected for the floor timber. The same is true of the side frame on the left of the frame next in line. The planks of the bottom lie side by side, while those of the walls overlap. All are fastened to the frames, not to each other.

built in their traditional fashion have been discovered, for example, in London and at Zwammerdam itself. But there was obviously a local method of shipbuilding that native craftsmen preferred to follow.

The Zwammderdam and related vessels are all long and narrow; they carried no sail and were propelled by oars alone. The shape shows that, despite their massive planking, they were for use on rivers and other sheltered waters. But there were also vessels that were pure sailing craft and built with the strength to handle the boisterous open waters off northern Europe. No remains have been found, but we know of them through a description in Caesar's *Gallic Wars*. In 56 BC, in the course of his conquest of Gaul, Caesar decided to subdue the Veneti, a people who lived in Brittany. He quickly discovered that they had a foolproof defence: they simply took to their boats and sailed out to where his legionaries could not reach them. The upshot was a bitter naval battle between his fleet of warships, all standard low and light galleys, and the ships of the Veneti, which, he reports, were totally different. For

> they build the hulls with somewhat flatter bottoms than our craft to make it easier to go through the shallow depths of low tide and over the shoals; they build prow and stern up rather high to handle the size of the waves when a sea is running; and they use oak throughout to withstand any amount of violent pounding. Beams are of timbers a foot square made fast with iron nails an inch thick, and anchors are held by iron chain instead of rope. Their sails are of hide or softened leather instead of linen, possibly because they have no flax and do not know how to use it, but more likely because they think linen will not stand up to the violence of ocean storms and the force of the winds there and will not drive such heavy vessels efficiently. In a clash with a fleet of these craft the only advantages our boats had were their speed and the fact that they were driven by oars; in every respect the enemy's type of ship was better suited and adapted for these waters with their strong winds.[1]

Flat bottoms, massive timbers of oak, heavy nails – these are the distinguishing characteristics of the craft found at Zwammerdam and elsewhere in northern Europe. For a while it looked as if these very characteristics might enable the Veneti to survive the Roman attack on them, for the ponderous oak planking was so obviously impervious to the Romans' chief threat, a blow of the ram, that Caesar's commanders did not even try any. Moreover, the lofty sterns gave the Veneti the advantage in exchanges of missiles, since men stationed there were able to fire their volleys down upon the low Roman craft. The Romans ultimately found the key to victory in an improvised tool for disabling the enemy's rigging – sharp sickles lashed to long poles. They would send a galley dashing alongside one of their opponents' lumbering ships, and, reaching up with these improvised cutters, slash the lines holding the sail-yard, causing it to fall. Two or three galleys would then surround the vessel, immobile and helpless, and the legionaries would swarm aboard for the kill.

Colour Plate XI Gaily painted Roman pleasure yacht. Wall painting from a Roman building now in the Museo Nazionale Romano. Early 1st century AD.

Colour Plate XII Detail of a scene showing the Nile in flood. The river spills over the land on each side of its banks; here a man in a reed canoe poles his way through the shallow waters of the overflow. Mosaic in the Palazzo Barberini, Palestrina, Italy. Early 1st century BC.

S MARCVS
CLERVS · PPLS ·

Colour Plate XIII Cogs in action. Note the high sides, the straight line of the stem and stern, and the sharp angle at which these meet the keel. Illustration from a manuscript in the British Library (Roy. 10 E IV, fol. 19). 14th century AD.

Colour Plate XIV The crew of a Mediterranean three-masted lateener, carrying the corpse of St Mark from Alexandria to Venice, drop the sails as they approach the shore. Detail of a mosaic in the Basilica of St Mark, Venice; 12th century AD.

The next notable step in north European shipbuilding took place in Scandinavia. Here, in the early centuries of the first millennium AD, shipwrights started on the path that would lead to the craft with which the Vikings gained their maritime fame.

The hallmark of the Viking ship is the way in which the planks were laid: it was, as we noted earlier (Chapter 3), clinker-built or, to use a synonymous and more self-evident term, lapstrake, that is, the strakes, as the full runs of planking from stem to stern are called, did not meet edge to edge but each upper strake overlapped the one below and the two were held together by fastenings through the double thickness. In the Zwammerdam boats the planks along the sides were set this way but 108 were fastened to side frames, not to each other. At Halsnøy, south of Bergen in Norway, there were found fragmentary remains, dating to the second century AD, of planks set lapstrake and sewn together, that is, they had holes drilled where the thickness was double, through which some form of cord must have passed. The earliest fully preserved example of a clinker-built vessel dates from several centuries later, sometime between AD 350 and 400, and is a superb specimen of shipbuilding; the shipwrights of the age had made impressive progress. It was excavated almost a century and a half ago from a bog at Nydam in Schleswig, north 109 Germany, where it had perhaps been ritually deposited in celebration of a victory in battle. It is a long, narrow and low open war galley, with a length of some 78 feet, a maximum beam of 10 feet, and a depth amidships of 4 feet (24 × 3 × 1.3 m). There were fifteen rowers to a side,

109 The Nydam boat. Second half of the 4th century AD.

110 In this photograph, taken in 1929, a Swedish shipwright is finishing a clinker-built hull. He has completed the shell of planking and prepared the frames that will be inserted in it; his next step will be to fasten the frames to the planking.

and these may have been the sole form of propulsion, since no fittings for a mast were found. Instead of a keel there was a central bottom plank, on each side of which rose nine other planks in a shallow graceful arc. All were of oak. Set lapstrake, they were fastened to each other by a line of iron rivets that passed through the double thickness. What is particularly striking is that each plank, over 80 feet long and 20 inches wide (about 24 × 0.5 m), was one solid piece of oak; we can only marvel at the skill of the teams that fashioned them out of huge tree trunks. The hull was stiffened by the insertion, at three-foot intervals, of frames made out of naturally curved pieces of timber which were lashed to cleats formed by the cutting away of the inside surface of the planks. The frames had been inserted after the planks had all been put in place, for clinker-built craft, 110
like those of the Mediterranean, were constructed shell-first (Chapters 3, 9). A single steering oar was found, which no doubt was carried on the starboard quarter; this is different from Mediterranean practice, where ships were fitted with two steering oars, one on each quarter. Long and narrow lines, shallow draft, overlapping planks secured by iron rivets, a single steering oar – these were to be the distinguishing characteristics of the Viking galley.

The next example of a vessel so built, dating to the early decades of the seventh century, is the famed ship found at Sutton Hoo in Suffolk – 111
or, rather, the ghost of a ship. The site was the final resting place of an

aristocrat, very likely a king, who had been buried in a ship, as was common practice in many parts of the Scandinavian world at the time (manifold explanations have been offered as to why such a burial should turn up in East Anglia). The wood, lying in damp and acid soil, had almost totally disintegrated, but had left a perfect picture of itself in the form of a dark stain against the yellow sand that had been piled around the hull, and the lines of rivets, though turned to rust, stood out perfectly. The Sutton Hoo craft was bigger than the Nydam, almost 100 feet long with a maximum beam of 16 feet (about 30 × 4.8 m), but it had been made in the same general way, with overlapping planks held together by iron rivets and braced internally by widely spaced frames. It, too, was propelled by oarsmen, twenty to a side. There were some differences: the strakes were not solid but composed of several pieces that had been joined together, with small rivets pinning the joints, and the frames had been cut zigzag fashion on the underside to fit snugly against the overlapped planks, and had been treenailed, not lashed, to them.

The Sutton Hoo ship brings us into the world of Viking craft, for many of the remains of these reflect not only the same shipbuilding tradition but the same religious tradition: they, too, come from ship-burials. And for Viking craft we finally have at our disposal written sources to supply some historical background and enable us to determine the roles they played. The Ferriby boats could well have been used for river and coastal trade, but we have no idea of what that trade was like, and the same is true of the Zwammerdam boats. The vessel found at Nydam was a war galley, but there are no clues as to who manned it and what battles they engaged in. But we know very well how the Vikings used their boats.

From at least the later part of the eighth century on into the ninth and tenth, marauders from Denmark and Norway descended upon the coastal towns of the British Isles and northern France, at first merely to raid and run but soon to ferry in forces that established permanent settlements. This called for galleys that were shallow enough to nose up to a beach, big enough to carry powerful bands of armed men, and at times horses as well, and swift enough to outstrip pursuers.

Thanks to the discovery over a century ago, in 1880, of a well-preserved ship-burial at Gokstad in southern Norway that dates from about AD 112
850, we have a good idea of what a typical Viking galley looked like and how it was built. Unlike the finds at Nydam and Sutton Hoo, the Gokstad ship was definitely designed to be sailed as well as rowed. It has a proper keel, and on it amidships is a heavy keelson in which the mast was stepped. The vessel is 78 feet in length, 16 ft 9 in. at its widest, and 6 ft 9 in. deep amidships (23 × 5.1 × 2 m). It was clearly intended for use in open water, for the oars were not worked over the gunwale but through ports in the side, the freeboard had been raised by two lines of strakes above the line of ports, and the ports themselves were fitted with ingeni-

111 The Sutton Hoo ship (early 7th century AD) as it appeared in 1939. The lines of the planks and the line-up of rivets are clearly visible.

ously pivoted shutters to close them off when travelling under sail in rough seas. The planks, of oak, are riveted to each other in the usual fashion. Spanning the hull at three-foot intervals are floor timbers over the bottom and crossbeams two feet above the keel; the floor timbers, as on the Nydam boat, are lashed to cleats protruding from the planks and their upcurving ends meet the ends of the crossbeams, which are fastened to them. Over the crossbeams were laid loose planks to form a deck. There are no signs of benches for the rowers; perhaps they lashed their sea chests to the deck and sat on them. There were sixteen oars a side, each about 17 ft 6 in. (5 m) long. On the starboard quarter was a 10-foot (3 m) steering oar turned by a horizontal tiller socketed in the handle. The mast, of pine, was probably about 40 feet (12 m) high, could be unshipped and lowered, and carried a tall squaresail.

The Gokstad ship, with a length to beam ratio of about 4.5 to 1, was probably intended to carry goods rather than warriors. A ship-burial at Ladby on the Danish island of Fünen has yielded the remains of a much more slender galley with a ratio of 7.1 to 1; this no doubt was a man-of-war, though a relatively small one with but a dozen oars to a side. Viking warships were often long enough to accommodate double that number. The biggest on record, the *Long Dragon* of Olaf Tryggvason, a king of Norway who ruled about AD 1000, had thirty-four rowers a side and was probably all of 140 feet (42.6 m) in length.

In 1956 a discovery was made in Roskilde Fjord, twenty miles or so west of Copenhagen, that provides an idea of the range of Viking craft. Sometime around AD 1000 five vessels had been filled with stones and sunk across the fjord where the village of Skuldelev now stands, to block the approach by water to the town of Roskilde. The ships were excavated and their wood treated for preservation; the remains are now on view in a museum at Roskilde. Two were warships. One of these measured 60 feet in length and 8 in beam (18.3 × 2.4 m). The other was much longer, over 90 feet (27 m), and very likely just as slender, but not enough was preserved to reveal its actual width. Long narrow craft like these or the Ladby ship were surely what the Vikings used for their raids on the British Isles and the northern coast of France; they are the reality behind the vessels pictured in the famous Bayeux tapestry. Of the other vessels found off Roskilde, two were merchant galleys. One, a small coaster 113
about 45 feet long and 10 feet 6 inches wide (13.7 × 3.2 m), i.e., a length to beam ratio of 4.2 to 1, had an open hold amidships where the mast stood and cargo was stowed; there were ports for five oars forward of this space and two aft. The other was bigger and heavier, 54 feet long and 15 wide (16.5 × 4.6 m), and more powerfully built with stout frames. It had an open hold amidships and decks fore and aft. Most probably it carried very few oars and depended almost wholly on sail. Quite possibly it was in this kind of ship that the Vikings made their bold open-water voyages to Iceland, Greenland and America.

112 ABOVE The Gokstad ship. About AD 850.

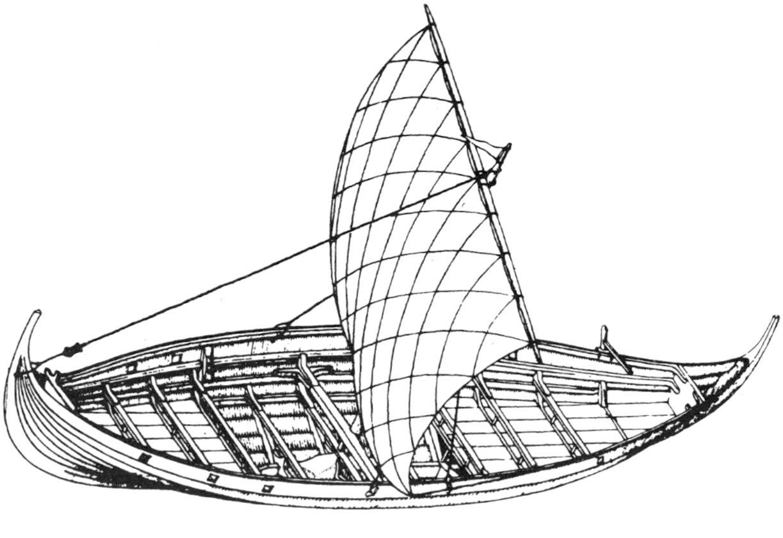

113 Reconstruction of a small merchant galley found at Roskilde. About AD 1000.

But it did not monopolise the trade of the North Sea and Baltic. Here another, distinctly different, type of merchantman shared the waters, the cog.

The Viking style of ship was all elegant rounded curves; the cog was XIII
all inelegant straight lines and angles. It had a flat bottom, a straight stem and stern, both of which met the keel at an angle, and high stiff sides. There were no oars, just a single mast and sail. With such lines, it was undoubtedly far slower than the types of merchantmen found, for 113
example, at Roskilde; on the other hand, its box-like shape provided more space for cargo than in a rounded hull. And its flat bottom enabled it to deliver its cargo wherever there was a beach: it would sail in when the tide was dropping, unload when left high and dry, and float off when the tide flooded in again. What is more, the high stiff sides were a good defence against attack: raiders found these very hard to scale from their low galleys, especially in the face of a hail of missiles from crossbowmen firing down from a cog's lofty rail.

The cog's construction was as unusual as its lines. The flat bottom was smooth, made up of a keel plus planks set edge to edge lengthwise and fastened to floor timbers laid across them. But the sides, rising stiffly at an angle from the bottom, were clinker-built. The cog was made, in other words, exactly like the Zwammerdam boats described above. Poss- 108
ibly there was a direct line of development between the two, the cog being a form developed for use on the open waters of the North Sea.

For, so far as we can tell, the cog came into being among the Frisians, the people who inhabited the southern coast of the North Sea from, roughly, the mouth of the Rhine in Holland to the mouth of the Weser in north-western Germany. The tidal flats along these shores were an ideal locale for such a boat. It made its appearance at least as early as the seventh century AD; its use soon spread, and ultimately, between 1200 and 1400, it was to be seen in all the major ports of the North Sea and the Baltic. Then it succumbed, like so many other craft of the age, to the fundamental changes in ship construction and rigging that the fifteenth century ushered in.

12
A New Age

Throughout the whole of ancient times, up to, say, the middle of the first millennium AD, seagoing merchantmen of the Mediterranean were built, rigged, and steered the same way. They were built shell-first with planks fastened edge to edge by means of multiple mortise and tenon joints and with frames inserted into the shell; they were rigged with squaresails; and they were steered by side rudders, a large oar mounted on each quarter. Similarly, until well past the end of the first millennium AD, the seagoing merchantmen of the north were built, rigged and steered the same way. They too were constructed shell-first but with the planks overlapping each other, not set edge to edge, and fastened by rivets and nails through the double thickness; their rig was a single big squaresail; and they were steered by a single side rudder, a large oar mounted on the starboard quarter.

In the second half of the first millennium AD, the Mediterranean merchantman began to see changes. The most obvious is the increasing number rigged with lateen sails. The lateen had been in use since at least 90
the second century AD, but only on small craft. Now larger ships began to carry it and there were even three-masted lateeners. In construction XIV
shipwrights gradually moved from the shell-first to the skeleton-first method; the discovery of the Serçe Liman wreck reveals that by the time it was built, about AD 1025, the transition had been completed (see Chapter 9).

The north was more resistant to change. Its seagoing merchantmen continued to be clinker-built, to be rigged with a single large squaresail, and to be steered with a single side rudder. But then, sometime around the end of the twelfth century, came one of the major developments in maritime history – the introduction of that simple but supremely efficient piece of nautical equipment, the rudder hinged to the stern of a vessel, not mounted on its quarter. Nobody knows who or even what country deserves the credit; all we can say is that it first appears in pictures of northern ships dating from around the end of the twelfth century. As a matter of fact, northern seamen had to invent the stern rudder or some- 114
thing similar as soon as they began to venture into open water aboard ships that, like the merchantmen found at Roskilde, depended largely or solely on sail. A sailing vessel will sooner or later find itself forced to angle into the direction of the wind, and on such a course, under the pressure of the wind, it will tend to heel over. A northern craft, if heading into a strong wind from starboard, might heel over so far that its single steering oar would be lifted out of the water. With a rudder hinged to the stern there was no such danger. Very likely cogs or vessels similar in shape XIII
were the first to carry it, for attaching it to their stiff and straight stern would have been as easy as hinging a door to its post, whereas attaching it to Viking craft, which were as rounded at the stern as at the prow, would have called for considerable adaptation. The Mediterranean, where ships carried a side rudder to port as well as starboard and hence had less of a

114 An early example of a stern rudder. Detail of a relief on the font in Winchester Cathedral. Second half of the 12th century AD.

problem with heel, took its time in adopting the new device, but by the fifteenth century it had become universal there as well.

Then, in the latter half of the fifteenth century, came the change that was to revolutionise the sailing ship – the mounting of squaresails, one above the other, on the same mast. And in its wake came the vessel that was to dominate the seas for the next four centuries, the full-rigged ship with its three masts and superimposed sails.

Three-masted vessels were by no means new: they had been seen 82
in the Mediterranean from the third century BC onward. Nor were superimposed sails totally new: by the first century AD, the Romans had at least one form, a small triangular topsail above the main. But for 84
centuries thereafter no further advances took place. In the Mediterranean, the lateen became the favoured sail, and lateen sails cannot be superimposed. In the north, shipbuilders rigged their craft, from the sleek Viking galleys to the lumbering cogs, with a single mast carrying one large square mainsail – and this even found favour in the Mediterranean. During the twelfth and thirteenth centuries northern ships carrying Crusaders to the Holy Land were to be seen passing through, and the shipwrights of Genoa and Venice and other maritime centres became aware that the rig borne by these vessels had certain advantages over their own lateeners: it required, for example, a much smaller crew. So they too began to build square-riggers, including, by the middle of the fifteenth century, versions big enough to be fitted with three masts.

Then came the revolutionary development – the superimposing of sails. By the end of the century a topsail had been added to the foremast and the mainmast to produce the earliest version of the full-rigged ship.

It had a basic suit of six sails: a bowspritsail on a short spar jutting over the prow, two superimposed squaresails on the foremast, two on the mainmast, and a single lateen sail on the mizzenmast. A short suit of five took Columbus to the New World (his *Santa Maria* had no topsail on the foremast); the full suit took Da Gama to India and Magellan around the world. As time passed, masts rose higher and more and more sails were added until, by the nineteenth century, the culmination was reached with the soaring masts and multiple levels of canvas on the clippers that raced home with tea from the Far East or wool from Australia.

Hand in hand with this vital development in rigging went an equally vital development in shipbuilding. Indeed, the two were interconnected: it took bigger and more powerful hulls to support the expanded rigging, and it took the expanded rigging to furnish sufficient drive to move the heavier hulls. What made such hulls possible was the switch from the shell-first method of construction to the skeleton-first. In the Mediterranean, as we have seen, shipbuilders were using the new technique by 1025. It soon made its way to the north for the construction of large merchantmen (boatwrights there long clung to the traditional lapstrake construction for small craft).

The skeleton-first method very likely first recommended itself because of the savings it produced in materials and manpower: no longer did big chunks of log have to be cut away as waste in order to shape the planks sufficiently to take the required curves; no longer did the shipwrights have to spend endless hours fashioning and fitting thousands of mortise and tenon joints. But there were more important advantages going well beyond mere savings in costs. Building skeleton-first not only permitted infinitely more flexibility in the design of hulls but also the capability of making them far larger and at the same time relatively lighter and stronger. Vessels in the future would run the gamut of shape and size, from the stubby and roly-poly Dutch flute to the long and elegantly slender American clipper. And they would gain for the West dominion over the seas throughout the age of the wooden ship.

Bibliography

BASCH, L., *Le musée imaginaire de la marine antique* (Athens 1987). A comprehensive review, with over 1100 illustrations, of ancient representations of ships and boats.

BASS, G. (ed.), *A History of Seafaring Based on Underwater Archaeology* (London 1972). A survey of underwater finds dating from the earliest times to this century.

CASSON, L., *The Ancient Mariners* (2nd edn, Princeton 1991). A survey of the maritime history of the ancient world.

CASSON, L., *Ships and Seamanship in the Ancient World* (2nd edn, Princeton 1986). A study, with full documentation of source material, of ancient naval technology.

GIANFROTTA, P., and POMEY, P., *Archeologia subacquea: storia, tecniche, scoperte e relitti* (Milan 1980). A comprehensive review of the techniques of marine archaeology and the finds in the Mediterranean dating to the ancient period.

GREENHILL, B., *Archaeology of the Boat* (London 1976). The first half treats primitive boats, the second half the evolution of watercraft in northern Europe.

JOHNSTONE, PAUL, *The Sea-Craft of Prehistory* (Cambridge, Mass. 1980). A worldwide survey of prehistoric craft.

MORRISON, J., and COATES, J., *The Athenian Trireme* (Cambridge 1986). A comprehensive study of warships and warfare of the fifth and fourth centuries BC. Two final chapters describe in detail the building of the replica of an Athenian trireme.

MORRISON, J., and WILLIAMS, R., *Greek Oared Ships 900–322 B.C.* (Cambridge 1968). A detailed study of the ships of the period accompanied by a catalogue, with many illustrations, of all representations.

PRYOR, J., *Geography, Technology, and War. Studies in the maritime history of the Mediterranean, 649–1571* (Cambridge 1988). A study of the geographical and meteorological factors and their effect on all phases of maritime history.

Notes

1 The Birth of the Boat
1. Herodotus 1.194.
2. Caesar, *De Bello Civile,* 1.54.
3. Marco Polo, Bk I, ch. XVIII, trans. H. Yule (3rd edn, London 1903, I, p. 108).

2 Egypt
1. Herodotus 2.96.
2 J. Breasted, *Ancient Records of Egypt* (Chicago 1906), I, nos 428–32.

3 Ancient Shipbuilding
1. *Odyssey* 5.247–53.

5 The Warship
1. J. Pritchard, *Ancient Near Eastern Texts* (2nd edn, Princeton 1955), 228.
2. Ibid. 239.
3. S. Mercer, *The Tell El-Amarna Tablets* (Toronto 1939), no. 114.
4. Ibid., no. 98.
5. Pritchard (see n. 1 above), 263.

6 The Age of the Trireme
1. Thucydides 1.13, 1–2.
2. Aristophanes, *The Frogs,* 1074.
3. Thucydides 6.31, 3.
4. Ibid. 8.45, 2.
5. Ibid. 8.95, 4.
6. Xenophon, *Hellenica,* 2.1, 27.
7. Ibid. 2.1, 28.
8. Thucydides 7.70, 4–6.

7 The Age of the Supergalleys
1. Plutarch, *Demetrius,* 43.5.
2. Athenaeus 5.203e–204b.
3. Polybius 16.3.

8 Winning with Fire
1. Leo, *Naumachica,* 6.
2. Ibid. 69.

9 Merchantmen
1. Lucian, *Navigium,* 5.
2. Acts 27.29.
3. Athenaeus 206f–207b.
4. Ibid. 208e–f.
5. Ibid. 209a–b.
6. Lucian, *Navigium,* 5–6.
7. Libanius, *Orationes,* 1.31.
8. Philo, *In Flaccum,* 26.
9. Acts 27.6.
10. Ibid. 27.31.

10 Along the Coasts, in Harbours, on Rivers
1. Synesius, *Epistolae,* 4.160a.
2. Ibid. 160b–c.
3. Ibid. 160c.
4. Ibid. 162c–164a.

11 In the North
1. Caesar, *De Bello Gallico,* 3.13.

List of Illustrations

Index